What readers are saying:

"Thank you for sharing *A Glimpse of My Heart*. It is such an appropriate title. And your love, empathy and professionalism are on every page...It's a wonderful gift to share." (Linda Cathey RN OCN, Clinical Supervisor Outpatient Oncology Services)

"l would laugh out loud at times...the daughter-in-law that was Labenese--and cry with stories like Joe. I went back to work with a renewed sense of what it was to be an oncology nurse...With reading your book, it wasn't just me struggling to make sense of it all, I was part of a greater good with all (nurses caring for cancer patients) having the same feelings...

I wanted to thank you because your book gave me the courage...to focus back on the human element. I made a difference and that made me feel like I was doing the right thing...I left feeling fulfilled...like I finally figured it out.

Thanks so much for a glimpse into your soul. It helped me re-evaluate the kind of nurse I want to be and gave me personal healing. I REALLY needed that. Words can't express how much I needed that."(Kimberly Peterson RN)

"It is a wonderful tribute to our Nursing Profession and a great read. It makes you laugh and makes you cry." (Peggy Sorenson RN OCN)

"If you are a nurse, read this and remember why you go to work. If you are a human, read it and be glad there are people like Delraya." (Marian Wilson MPH RN)

A Glimpse of My Heart

— ONE NURSE'S STORY —

Delraya Anstine RN OCN

BALBOA.
PRESS

A DIVISION OF HAY HOUSE

Balboa Press books may be ordered through booksellers or by contacting:

Balboa Press
A Division of Hay House
1663 Liberty Drive
Bloomington, IN 47403
www.balboapress.com
1-(877) 407-4847

Because of the dynamic nature of the Internet, any web addresses or links contained in this book may have changed since publication and may no longer be valid. The views expressed in this work are solely those of the author and do not necessarily reflect the views of the publisher, and the publisher hereby disclaims any responsibility for them.

ISBN: 978-1-4525-4543-1 (sc)
ISBN: 978-1-4525-4545-5 (hc)
ISBN: 978-1-4525-4544-8 (e)

Library of Congress Control Number: 2012900543

The author of this book does not dispense medical advice or prescribe the use of any technique as a form of treatment for physical, emotional, or medical problems without the advice of a physician, either directly or indirectly. The intent of the author is only to offer information of a general nature to help you in your quest for emotional and spiritual well-being. In the event you use any of the information in this book for yourself, which is your constitutional right, the author and the publisher assume no responsibility for your actions.

Any people depicted in stock imagery provided by Thinkstock are models, and such images are being used for illustrative purposes only.
Certain stock imagery © Thinkstock.

Printed in the United States of America

Balboa Press rev. date: 2/7/2012

Dedication

This book is dedicated to my stepfather, Orwin Evenson, who passed away on February 20, 2010 after a six year battle with chondrosarcoma that slowly took many parts of his body.

Sarcoma is a cancer that develops in tissues, such as bone or muscle. Chondrosarcoma is a type of cancer that grows in cartilage cells, the connective tissue from which bones are created.

My book would not be complete without telling Orwin's courageous story.

10 percent of the proceeds of this book will go toward finding a cure for Sarcoma.

Introduction

"Mom, I have lots of words in my head!" That's what my daughter would say to me when she was four or five. Then she really needed to talk to me, and I would stop what I was doing to listen. That is why I am writing these stories. I have so many words in my head that need to be expressed. In just one day, a multitude of incredible things happen at such a rapid pace that there is not enough time to digest each moment. It is difficult to keep my emotions in check as it is not uncommon to go from a room in which a patient has just died to another where a patient is doing well and possibly getting his first chemotherapy treatment. It is necessary to stay calm in a crisis when you really feel like screaming. Writing these events down helps me to reflect on them, digest them, make sense of them, and grow from them.

These are my stories. Another nurse might see the same situation in a completely different way, and I know that each nurse has his or her own unique stories. Some of the facts have been changed to maintain patient privacy.

The trend these days seems to focus on the dramatic, fast paced and exciting aspects of the medical field. But there are so many deeply moving dramas in every aspect of health care. These are the stories of real people. Some are quiet and subtle and touching; some are bold and loud and the battle goes on for months or years. In all cases, people in general, including patients, family, and friends never cease to amaze me with their strength, courage and tenacity.

I would like to thank the many people who have touched and motivated me. Among those are the nurses that I have worked with over the years. Not only are you consistently committed to compassion but you bring your own unique gifts to your profession. I have learned so much from you all.

Special thanks to Linda Cathey RN OCN Clinical Supervisor of Outpatient Oncology services, Peggy Sorenson RN OCN, Kimberly Peterson RN, Carol Reager RN, Wynda Dobler RN, Marian Wilson MPH RN and Mary Nierenberg (a dear friend that passed away just three years ago from a heart attack) for your support and encouragement with this project, and a couple of nurses that were monumental role models in my early nursing career, Polly Parisot RN and Mary Ann McHugh RN.

Also, thank you to our oncologists. Your brilliance and commitment to patients is phenomenal.

Thank you to my Grandma Celeste. You told me that I could accomplish anything I set out to do and I believed you.

Thank you to my daughter, Christie, and son, Jeff, who have allowed me to feel love (and pain) beyond anything I could have ever imagined. When you are happy, I am rejoicing, when you are hurting, my pain is almost unbearable. Seeing you grow into caring intelligent adults, and see what amazing parents you both are has been among my greatest gifts. I know each of you will continue to touch the world in your own unique ways.

This book was written for both of you with so much love, that you might know me a little more deeply. I hope that you can pass some of these stories on to your children so they can know a little more about who their grandma really was.

Most of all, I would like to thank my husband Rich. After 40 years together my love for you only grows deeper. Thank you for your support all these years; all the papers you have proofread, and the long hours you have worked to provide for your family. You are a common thread in all my stories. You are a kind, moral, smart and handsome man and an outstanding father and grandfather.

My goal in my nursing career, as well as in this book is that as we serve our fellow man so we might come to know ourselves better.

My wish and prayer for each person as they read this is that God will keep you safe and healthy in mind, body, and spirit and that you live the passions of your heart, are mindful of the miracles that occur every day and see the divine in all situations.

Table of Contents

The Why

Many people have asked me over the years why I chose to be a nurse. I would have to say that I feel nursing is pure and genuine. It is dealing with people at a gut level; human being to human being. When people learn that you are a nurse, they so trustingly open up their lives to you. It is an honored opportunity to assist people in the battle to regain their health, or deal with an acute or chronic illness.

An oncology nurse cares for patients who have been diagnosed with cancer. It involves many aspects; helping a person deal with the traumatic news that they have the disease, the administration of chemotherapy treatments along with monitoring and treating related side effects, and dealing with end of life issues when the treatments fail or are no longer effective.

I have been an oncology nurse for twenty three years, thirteen of those in an acute care inpatient hospital unit and ten years in busy outpatient clinics.

When I tell people that fact, it is usually elicits a sigh followed by a look of sadness. I want to say, yes, it can be sad sometimes but I feel so passionate about what I can do and the changes I can make in people's lives. I love being an oncology nurse. It is exhilarating, complex and ever changing. Most days I am challenged to the max physically, intellectually, emotionally and spiritually with all that there is to be done, but what an opportunity that is to discover the best person you are meant to be!

And of course, oncology patients are among the most strong and endearing, each fighting their unique battles, giving back so much more than we are able to give them. They (along with their loved ones) become like our families. As hospital nurses, we work so hard for them all the way from achieving adequate pain control, down to getting fresh grapes from the kitchen if that sounded good to a patient on a particular day. As clinic nurses, we do our best to show our hopefulness for the greatest outcome by our positive presence day to day.

I have learned so much about myself and about life from being in this field. The small battles are as important as, or even more so than the larger ones and each day should be so cherished. Most people forget this unless they or someone close to them see their own mortality staring them in the face.

I see *daily* the value of every *minute* and how hard people will fight for it. I have learned to live life more passionately and am less afraid to take risks than I used to be. I can become enthralled with the ocean waves grasping for the shore. I can be moved to tears by a spectacular sunset, the melody of a song, or soft kisses from my grandchildren; and laugh whether it is from a good joke or simply from the absurdities of life.

The following are a compilation of stories from my 23 year nursing career; about the becoming and the being. So many stories I didn't capture on paper and now all the details run together, and also other stories are too private to share, but here is a glimpse from my perspective of what it is like to be in this profession.

Penguins?

Dr. Doom, Piranha and Land Shark

Throughout my nursing education, I thought the three people listed above were my worst nightmares.

Dr. Doom was my Anatomy and Physiology instructor. A&P was a year long course that could put fear in the bravest of souls. Why did he make us learn every little detail? Why was there so much material? Why were his tests so difficult? Maybe he really was a super villain and a brilliant scientist whose experiments had gone wrong and now he had turned to making potential nurses' lives miserable.

Piranha was a nickname we gave one of our nursing instructors. She was a snappy attractive woman whom I admired a great deal but seemed to voraciously attack in the clinical setting. You could not please her. No matter how you prepared or how you cared for your patient, it was never enough. She graded extremely hard too. An A from her was almost an impossibility. It seemed that she wanted to eat us alive.

One day as about four of us nursing students sat in post clinical conference with Piranha, she said to us, "I was just about to say something really profane but I can't remember exactly how I was going to put it." We all were terrorized thinking we had done terribly that day and sat waiting to be cursed out, but it turned out that she was thinking instead of something very *profound* to say. We were all relieved at her slip of the tongue.

And lastly there was *Land Shark*. A Land Shark is defined as the cleverest of all sharks, unlike the great white shark, which tends to inhabit the waters and harbors and recreational beach areas, the

Land Shark may strike at any place and at any time and generally preys on young nursing students.

She was also a very intelligent attractive lady, but in clinical she would appear out of nowhere and at the least opportune time just when you thought you were safe and want to know what you were doing and why you were doing it. But instead of the *Baaa bump Baaa bump* as when a shark was approaching, one would hear the faint *click click click* of her heels that would gradually become louder and louder, and then you would see that flash of her eyes and you would know you were a goner.

As I look back on these three individuals, I now am thankful for them. They knew what was ahead for us. Human beings are not perfect and they do make mistakes. But in nursing there is no room for mistakes. It is a field where excellence is an expectation. They were pushing us to our max because they knew what lay ahead for us in the real world. Know the facts, think fast, stay sharp, stay on your toes in all situations and try so hard for perfection.

NORTH IDAHO COLLEGE

to the top of the mountain !

NURSING CLASS OF
1988
CAPPING

Delraya and husband Rich

Sound Track for
A Glimpse of My Heart
One Nurse's Story

Music is such an integral part of my life. If this book had a sound track, this is what it would be.

Side 1

Free Fallin'	Tom Petty
Lady	Kenny Rogers
If Tomorrow Never Comes	Garth Brooks
Love of My Life	Sammy Kershaw
Somewhere Over the Rainbow	Israel Kamakawiwo'ole
Smokey the Bear	Studio Group
Live Like You Were Dying	Tim McGraw
I Could Fly	Keith Urban

Side 2

All I Wanna Do	Sheryl Crow
Better Life	Keith Urban
Still Here	Natasha Bedingfield
Secret	Madona
These Boots are Made for Walkin'	Nancy Sinatra
Dancing Queen	Abba

Sound Track for A Glimpse of My Heart One Nurse's Story

Bad Day	Daniel Powter
Hit the Road Jack	Ray Charles
The Dance	Garth Brooks

Falling

There were two times that I almost decided to quit nursing school. This was one of them.

It was my first operating room clinical rotation as a nurse. I was around thirty years old, and had two small children at home. After getting my clinical preparations done which involved about three or four hours of research to prepare for the day, and getting the kids off to school, I ran out the door without breakfast and rushed to the hospital to find where I was supposed to be. I had butterflies, and was nervous to the point of being nauseous, and hadn't had much sleep the night before.

There are lots of rules in the OR. I scrubbed up according to protocol and gowned up according to regulations, and then entered the room where the surgery would take place. I was only there to observe, so there were certain places to stand and, *don't touch anything!* That was reiterated over and over by our instructors. While listening to the commotion in the operating room, it was obvious that everyone had their essential job to do...except me. I felt like I was just there to be in the way.

They brought a young woman in to have an abdominal hysterectomy. Everyone was ready. And with scalpel in hand, the doctor made a cut vertically down her belly. A tiny drop of blood trickled down from the cut as the tissue started to separate.

Suddenly my legs felt like jello, my head started to tingle, and then the room went black. That was the last thing I remembered. When I regained consciousness, I was lying on my side on a gurney out in the hall with a very soggy cool wet rag plastered on the back of my neck. Oh no, what had I done? I had passed out!! I felt horrified. What had happened in the operating room? Had I fallen right onto the sterile field and right onto the patient? I bet they are going to kick me out of the hospital and tell me to never come back, not to mention kick me out of nursing school. What did I think I was doing trying to be a nurse? I can't even handle a little blood. I am done!

Then someone came along to check on me. I can't recall exactly who. They suggested that I get up and go into the doctor's lounge and get some juice and find something to eat. Oh yes, that is exactly what I want to do. Go humiliate myself even more, and have all the doctors know what I had just done. I didn't have much choice though...so I went.

There were a few people in the lounge while I got something to eat and drink. And one kind doctor, Dr. Kent, began talking to me. I blurted out the whole story and he just smiled and said that he had passed out once and that actually many had at one time or another. He gave me some tips about breathing, wiggling my toes, and keeping my knees bent a little; and of course have something to eat and drink before hand. I thanked him for his kindness and told him I would try those things. Yes, yes, I would! Next time I was in the OR, I would definitely try all the things he had just said, some other day, some other time! He said no, not some other day. I needed to go right back in there, today, now. What? Go back in there and face the staff I had just humiliated myself in front of? But I wanted to be a nurse so badly, and be a good one; I didn't like feeling defeated, so I meticulously and thoroughly scrubbed again...and back into that room I went!

I ended up watching two more intense surgeries without any problems while applying Dr. Kent's techniques. The staff was very light-hearted about what had happened, and even said that it happened often. And I was relieved to learn that I hadn't fallen into the sterile field. It seemed that the anesthesiologist had seen me beginning to buckle, had scooped me up quickly, and taken me to the gurney in the hall.

That was about 23 years ago, and since that time, I have seen many intense situations and surgical procedures without any problems. It is just part of the job. Thank you Dr. Kent. In a big way I owe my career as a nurse to you.

NORTH IDAHO COLLEGE

Nursing Class 1988 Pinning

Dawn and Dusk

I had only been a nurse about a year and a half and had taken care of Mary often, watching her bravely fight her battle with metastatic breast cancer which was almost over. She was middle aged, too young to be dying I thought, as I stood beside her bed in the dark room thinking of the conversations we had had in the past. She was such a fighter. She had survived the sudden loss of her husband due to a heart attack only two years before. She told me how close they were and that their favorite song was Garth Brooks "If Tomorrow Never Comes." Toward the end she said she was looking forward to seeing her husband so she could tell him that she always knew how much he loved her even if he didn't say it often.

At that time, the oncology unit was right next to the nursery. Patients would love to walk down the hall to view the newborn infants through the window. Looking up on this day, however, I saw a very different site. A young man was pushing a bassinette on wheels toward Mary's room. He looked very determined. Even back then, rules were strict about leaving the obstetric area.

When he entered the room, he said to me that he had spent a lot of time thinking about this. "I don't know what you're going to say but I just want you to know that I'm going to do it anyway, no matter what you say. Mary has been a wonderful friend for a long time and has always done so much for us. I promised her when our baby was born she would get to see her and I'm going to keep that promise. I don't care what you say!" He barely took a breath. What could I say but, "Come in." He looked relieved while wheeling his new daughter in. He lifted the tiny perfect baby out and placed her in the crook of Mary's arm and said "Mary, this is our new daughter Emily. I promised you that you would meet her."

The squirming baby's rapid breathing interlaced with other sweet newborn sounds was in drastic contrast with the stiff body that held her. Mary's breaths were shallow and quiet with short periods where her breathing stopped altogether.

In these brief unexpected moments, I was viewing opposite ends of the spectrum, the circle of life, its never ending cycle. As Mary's sun was setting, Emily is a fresh dawn and hope for the future.

And I will hold to the hope that, in her adulthood, Emily won't have to worry about such things as breast cancer.

The Little Old Man

I caught him out of the corner of my eye walking up the hall. His steps were slow and heavy. The little old man whose hands were gnarled with arthritis now stood at the desk of the 3 North nursing station. It was early morning, the beginning of day shift and what looked to be a busy day. I was trying to gather all my information, thumbing through medical charts, finding current lab values, etc., and trying to prioritize the duties that lay ahead of me in the next 8 hours.

He stood there for a moment not saying anything as if he were trying to gather his composure. I looked up at him and met the saddest, kindest eyes I had ever seen, "My wife." He spoke slowly and then repeated. "My wife, do you remember her? Her name was Helen… Helen Smith. She was here a month ago in room 310. That is where she died. She had cancer. We were married 53 years."

My mind raced to recall the lady, and I felt frustrated that I couldn't. But instead of telling the truth, I said, "Oh yes, I remember her." With that I saw the old man begin to shake with sobs that seemed to rise from his very soul. I could do nothing but come from around the desk and hold him while he cried.

After a while, the sobs subsided. He talked a little about the past and his plans for the future. Then he said, "I think that I would like to be a volunteer here at the hospital. I can still do a lot of things you know." I said, "I think that is a very good idea." Then he said with a rather deep sigh. "Yes, yes. I think that is what I will do." With that he smiled, and said good-bye and walked away. His steps appeared a little lighter now as if his brief encounter with us had helped him to begin to heal and ease the heavy burden of grief he had been carrying.

I returned to the tasks at hand although my day now seemed a little richer and a little less cumbersome and I knew I would never forget the little old man with the kind eyes and the gnarled hands.

What loss cries for is not to be fixed
or to be explained,
But to be shared and, eventually, to
find its way to meaning."

"Those who are in trouble need a calmness of soul
from those who care for them.
We have to be able to look upon their distress
And allow them to bear it.
We can share their sadness;
We cannot fix their pain."

-Rabbi David Wolpe-

The Crabby Old Man

Of the thousands of patients I have cared for over the years, I have requested not to care for an individual only twice. This is one of those two times.

I have memories of a curmudgeonly gentleman that I attempted to care for one day when I was working on the medical floor. He was dying of respiratory disease from a lifetime of heavy smoking. His skin was paper thin with many tears and bruises from all the steroids he was taking to help him breathe, and yet still, he gasped for each breath.

He cursed me and criticized my every move. Although I tried to be patient and consider his condition, by late morning, I couldn't take any more of his verbal abuse. I talked to the charge nurse and explained to her how I felt. She was understanding and took over care of the patient herself. I found out that he had "gone through" all of the nurses that normally worked there, each refusing to take care of him. That is why she gave him to me, the float nurse, that day.

When the charge nurse entered his room, rather bluntly she told him that he was going to need people to take care of him and told him what he already knew, that he was getting toward the end of his life. But because of his meanness, he was running out of people who would care for him. It seemed harsh but in this situation necessary.

Toward the end of the shift, that same nurse encouraged me to go back into his room saying we both needed some resolution and closure to the situation. I didn't want to but did anyway.

As I entered the room, I saw a small man in the bed with great fears who had used his anger to squeeze out all other emotions. Although he did not apologize to me in words, his tone had softened. We talked for a short while as he told me about his difficult life and his fears of dying.

As I was leaving, I took a chance and gave him a quick hug to which he reciprocated and at that moment I was glad I had gone back to see him before leaving that day.

God bless you, crabby old man. God bless your broken spirit.

Lady

His name was Clyde. We all loved caring for him. He was a pleasant man with a gentle manner. He always had a kind word and a smile no matter how he was feeling. His leukemia required extremely aggressive treatment. We wished to support him through his ordeal although his age, other health problems, and past experiences with similar diagnoses made us have our doubts about the outcome.

His hospital stay was quite lengthy. He had his chemotherapy. Then the side effects began. Infections set in. Heart problems arose. It seemed that Clyde had more than his share of problems. He went to the coronary care unit then came back to oncology, then the intensive care unit and eventually back to us.

He had no family and had few visitors except for two neighbor ladies that came to see him frequently. They had taken a liking to him just as we all had.

Through all of Clyde's comings and goings, one constant remained; the picture that was placed tenderly at his bedside. We all made sure that it remained displayed and not tucked away with other belongings because we all knew how important it was to him. The photograph was of a sweet faced fuzzy black dog named Lady whose eyes glimmered with a feisty zest for life. Her coal black nose gleamed as it reflected the light and one might almost feel that by touching the photo, you would be able to feel its moistness. Lady had been Clyde's constant companion for quite some time and he loved to tell stories about her many antics.

As he grew weaker, the stories grew fewer. We all knew he was not winning his battle.

Frequently we would say, "You know Clyde is not getting any better. Wouldn't it be nice if he could see his dog one last time?" Then the day would become busy and days would run into other days as time was running out. Finally one Saturday, Clyde had slipped into unresponsiveness. Peggy was caring for him that day and she said, "I have something I need to work on today. Clyde needs to see his dog."

This didn't surprise me too much because aside from being one of my dearest friends, she is one of the best nurses I have ever seen, caring for her patients down to the most minute detail with expertise, love and compassion. Her commitment to what she believes, along with her generosity, radiate from her. One just feels good being around her.

Soon Peggy was on the phone talking to the hospital supervisor about her plan. I think that in this day and age we would have much more difficultly, but back then we were able to go ahead with our plan.

Peggy then talked to the kind neighbor lady who was caring for Clyde's precious companion. Arrangements were made and we all anxiously anticipated the arrival of our special guest.

After a while, the neighbor lady arrived, and on a leash a black dog with very white whiskers sauntered up the hall beside her. The dog looked old and tired but she seemed to perk up and wagged her tail when she entered the hospital room and caught her master's scent. We all followed the dog into the room and placed a soft flannel bath blanket on Clyde's bed and gently helped Lady up. She lay close to Clyde quietly whimpering and nuzzling his hand with her shiny wet nose. Although Clyde didn't appear to awaken, he seemed more peaceful than before, because, I believe he knew that Lady was with him.

Less than two hours later, Clyde passed away almost as if he were waiting to say goodbye to his special friend. A few days later we received a note from the neighbor lady which said, "Thank you for not just caring for Clyde but for caring about him too." I felt so extremely proud of the people I work with, and, as always, very proud to be an oncology nurse.

April First

After a couple of days off, I came back to work as charge nurse for the day shift on the 3 North oncology unit. Karen had been the night charge nurse, and as we sat at the nurse's station, she told me about the patients, including a brief report on each and any pertinent information that had happened during the night shift. She also told me how much staff I was entitled to for that day according to the complexity of care needed for our current patient population.

Karen started her long sordid report. They had a total of 15 patients and four were admitted to the unit during the night shift. One had been Bill, a longstanding patient who was in and out of the hospital frequently. He had circulation problems that have caused him to lose several toes and fingers and, a couple more she said were now turning black. He required dressing changes to those appendages every 2 hours, and he had a temperature of 103, and also was receiving numerous intravenous antibiotics throughout the day.

They had admitted a confused gentleman who kept trying to get out of bed and was incontinent of stool and urine, and a new leukemia patient who needed to start his first treatment this morning. A patient had accidently pulled out his central line. The surgeon would be coming in this morning to replace it, and he would need a nurse's assistance. On and on went the story.

Then she said, "Oh yeah, there were two sick calls last night so you are the only oncology nurse here today but John (our house supervisor who staffs for us) is calling everyone trying to find more nurses, but you may be short a nurse or two today. Oh, and John didn't have a nurse's assistant for the medical floor today so he took ours because the medical floor is full." While she nonchalantly told me her story, my head was reeling. "How was I going to pull this day off?" I thought. By the time she finished, my heart was pounding and I grabbed the phone to call John. "Boy, was a going to give him a piece of my mind!"

About that time, Karen burst out laughing just as all the night shift employees came from around the corner. They had all been hiding in the med room listening to our conversation. They all chimed together, "April Fools!!!!"

Congratulations you guys! That is the best (or worst) April Fool's joke ever played on me!

Hawaiian Days on 3 North

Peggy, Delraya, Teresa and Shari

Agape

After the morning report on all the patients, it appeared that I would have a busy but a feasible day. We were an acute care oncology unit, but also took care of many patients on an outpatient basis. I had three busy inpatients, and was assigned to one outpatient who was supposedly coming in for a quick intravenous infusion and would then be on his way.

When I first saw Tony, his wife Lynn was pushing him up the hall in a wheelchair. He was dark, husky, full-bearded man; in many ways reminding me of my own husband, so proud and very masculine. I'm sure he had been very independent not long ago.

After I introduced myself, I showed them to the outpatient room, while taking note that Tony was wearing a turtle shell brace. It is a two-pieced unit made of hard plastic that is attached together on the sides with Velcro strips that can be secured to fit tightly. It allows someone with a weak spine to be less likely to fracture vertebrae. In Tony's case, his bones were weak from progressive multiple myeloma, which is cancer of the bone marrow. As the cancer grows, it causes pain and destruction of the bones. Although the brace serves a valuable purpose, it is cumbersome, awkward, and difficult to manage. I also noted that he had a urinary catheter draining urine from his bladder into a Foley bag hooked onto his wheelchair.

And as always, I was checking out the veins in his arms trying to see if it was going to be difficult to start an IV for the hydration he would be getting. Eventually when people have the diagnosis of cancer, their veins get tired of all the poking and they just run and hide, or so it seems. Sometimes, it is very difficult to start an IV. As oncology nurses, we take pride in considering ourselves among the best at this skill, because our patients can be so challenging.

I was feeling fortunate that Tony was only there for quick hydration. One liter of D5½NS over one hour would be fairly easy to accomplish; then I could get back to my other patients. I felt it would be most efficient to just leave him in his wheelchair for the procedure.

My thoughts of a quick IV start and infusion soon went out the window. He told me that he needed his Foley catheter changed, needed a flu shot, a shot to build up his red blood cells and also wanted his chemotherapy. Additionally, he was on a tight time schedule. At a precise time, he had to catch a van that would accommodate his wheelchair, transporting him to his home, more than 60 miles away.

While I viewed this man and the total picture, and listened to all that he needed me to do, I felt annoyed at the time he would cost me, and concerned as to how I would manage the rest of my day. After 15 minutes and three people trying to get him into bed, followed by numerous phone calls to get doctors orders to try to achieve our goals, my stress level was beyond belief.

I started by putting warm moist towels on Tony's arms to help plump up his veins to help assure successful IV access, and then started working toward changing the catheter in his bladder.

But, while I spent time with this man and his wife, I began to feel something. "What was this presence in the room?" It seemed to float around me and settle in my soul allowing me to feel suddenly calm, light-hearted, and full of joy. While I tried somewhat awkwardly to maneuver his clothing to replace the catheter, and could feel Tony's kindness. He was lightly joking and gently teasing and appeared to be trying to make *me* feel comfortable. Here was a man who had lost all his independence and had to rely on others now for all things, and he appeared to be concerned with *my* feelings.

The afternoon wore on, and still, I could feel the unspoken respect and love between husband and wife. After I had completed all that needed to be done, Lynn put her arms around Tony, and again three of us now helped him back into the wheelchair so they could be on their way. Even as beads of perspiration dotted her brow, and in her breathless exhaustion, their feelings for each other were palpable. Their eyes met many times with a kind knowing smile crossing their faces almost as if to say, "We have both accepted what this outcome will be, but we will fight this battle to the very end with all the strength we can."

I believe that the presence in the room that day that softened my heart and eased the stressfulness was unconditional love. It allowed me to feel full, and peaceful, and light, and airy in the midst of all the stress. It is the type of love that says, "I will be here for you no matter what the circumstances." The Greek word for this kind of love is agape. It is the kind of love that God has for us that transcends words. As First Corinthians Chapter 13 states, "It is long suffering, it bears all things and endures all things. It never fails and will go on forever. Nothing can destroy it...not even death."

Code Blue

Here I stand in the hospital room. The resuscitation efforts after the Code Blue call have been unsuccessful. Everyone has gone almost as quickly as they had come it seems. Only seconds ago, the room was jammed full of people and equipment and so much activity that one could barely move. Now the silence is painfully loud.

The bed is pulled out from its normal place tucked next to the wall. Remnants of equipment and supplies are strewn everywhere. My patient is lying here in the stillness. His body is still warm, but his chest no longer rises and falls; and he has the unmistakable color of death. Adrenaline is still racing through me from all that has just happened. I am feeling shocked and am wondering how I am going to tell his family. Even though he has a terminal illness, this was so unexpected. They had not had time to prepare. I am thinking of how I will document all that has just occurred, and wondering how I will get the room back in order and make him presentable and appear peaceful before family members arrive.

What if I could rewind the clock several hours knowing what I now know? What if I could say to the family? "Don't go, now; stay with him. Tell him all the things you have always wanted to say. Express your love, your apologies, your regrets. This is his last night!"

But the crystal ball is not for me to peer into.

Was there something that I missed? Some clue that this was going to happen? My mind went over each detail of my physical assessment done just a short time earlier. Nothing could have indicated that this would have happened.

I remember a colleague telling me something a long time ago that has been a great comfort to me over the years. It goes something like: There is a fixed path that patients, and each of us are on. And, no matter what is done or not done, that course cannot be altered. The plan for ones life will progress or end according to the laws of the universe.

I contemplate all of these things while taking a deep breath and whispering a little prayer that I will find the right words to say to make my message somewhat bearable. I go to the phone and make the call; then straighten the room, prepare his body, and wait for the patients loved ones. *This is what I am here to do.*

Joe

I met him several years ago. I was assigned to be his nurse one day. He was handsome, polite and friendly. He was also 40, the same age that I was at that time. He said that they had found some spots of cancer and weren't sure where they had originated but that he was going to get some chemotherapy to take care of it.

As we talked about other things, I found that he had worked with my Mom at a grocery store few years earlier as a box boy and I told him that Mom was going to retire soon. Joe was kind and I had a pleasurable day caring for him. I didn't see or think of him for quite a while after that.

Then one day several months later, one of the other nurses asked me to give her a second opinion on a problem with an intravenous line she was having on one of her patients. I entered the room, told the patient what I was going to do and leaned over to look at the IV. Then I heard him say, "How does your mom like retirement?" I looked at him trying to recall the image of the man I had seen before. Instead, I saw a man that appeared to be in his seventies and quite thin (cachexic or emaciated are a couple of medical terms that better describe what I saw). I hoped that he didn't see the shock on my face. I said, "Joe, I didn't recognize you." He just said, "Yeah, I know. I've lost some weight." I left the room hoping he didn't see the tears in my eyes.

We saw him quite a bit after that. The cancer was in his liver but the doctors could not find where it originated which makes it difficult for doctors to find the right treatment plan. And now it just kept growing.

He just kept plugging away though, trying to make the best of things, and still went hunting with buddies when he could, and his friends did the best to accommodate him on these endeavors. They would bring photos of the trips that he couldn't go on so that he could still feel a part of things.

As time went on, things got tougher. The fluid from the cancer would build up in the peritoneal space around his stomach. It made him short of breath, nauseated and unable to eat. The doctor would have to insert a large needle to drain the fluid off. Sometimes he would remove four to five liters of fluid at a time. He would feel better for a while, but the fluid would always come back.

Up until the end of his life, he was always so friendly and maintained a sort of business as usual attitude. He would go outside to smoke several times a day no matter how bad he was feeling. He refused to have a nurse see him at home during the time he got to go home saying that his friends could help him. When he got to feeling too bad, he just wanted to be with us on the oncology unit.

Joe wrote in his journal daily up until the day he died. As he was writing one day, he read me a couple of entries. One talked of the procedure of drawing fluid off of his abdomen and how miserable he would be before, and even though it was painful, how much better he felt afterwards. He read another that said, "Today is April 1st. Happy April F*cking Fools Day!!!!" He thought that one was pretty funny!

Two days before he died was the last time he left his room to smoke. Family members were at his side and friends were coming to say goodbye. The day before he died, I went into his room. I wasn't assigned to be his nurse that day but I hugged his parents and took his hand. As he was lying so still with his eyes closed, I told him who I was and said that I had just stopped in to say hi and see how he was doing. I didn't expect much of a response but once again he shocked me. Without opening his eyes he said in a strong voice, "Hi," and called me by name. "I'm fine. Thanks for stopping by to see me." And once again I had tears in my eyes.

The next day when I came to work, the room was empty. He had died peacefully in the middle of the night with his family at his bedside. I wanted to cry but it would have to be later because there was a full assignment ahead of me and patients that needed to be cared for.

I hope Joe was able to look down and see how many lives he had touched and how many people cared so deeply about him, and… when I arrived home that night, my husband held me in his strong but tender arms and then it was time to cry.

Floating

The phone rang at 6:00 am. I was getting myself ready, expecting to work my normal day shift on the oncology unit just as I had the day before. It was John the house supervisor saying, "I need you to float to Coronary Care Unit today." When you are a hospital nurse, you have to expect to work in other areas when they are extra busy or when your own unit does not have many patients. I know it is part of my job but still my stress level goes up immensely. I am out of my area of expertise and thus out of my comfort zone. Also, it is hard to find things I need and get used to the routine of a different unit. But still, usually whenever I float I find that I have a very enlightening day. Today was to no exception. I was assigned to three very stable patients, with plenty of time to do my nursing care and time to do the things that make nursing seem rewarding and worthwhile, such as having the luxury to talk with and get to know them.

My first patient was a 68 year old gentleman named Hank. He had been in CCU for several days and had been admitted due to heart irregularities and severe shortness of breath. After a brief peek at my other two patients, I entered his room to assess him first because from report that morning I expected him to be the sickest of my three patients. There I found a very pleasant man who looked much older than his age. He had a history of diabetes and that of being a heavy smoker and from his looks, probably a heavy drinker also. He had had a bronchoscopy the day before in which they took a biopsy from a large mass in his right lung which had shown to be small cell lung cancer. Hank didn't know the results yet.

My assessment of him showed stable vitals with an EKG reading of chronic atrial fibrilation. His lungs were tight and wheezy with diminished breath sounds in the right lung fields. His skin was dusky gray and dry. He was also missing the two outer toes on his right foot. As I see a lot of people with missing digits, I am always curious to hear their story. He said that he guessed he had lost them because of his diabetes. He talked fondly of a daughter-in-law that always took him to his doctor's appointments and spoke sadly of an estranged son that he had not seen in 15 years who he thought might be living in New Mexico. The pulmonary doctor gave him the news about his lung cancer while I was seeing my other patients, but I talked with him shortly after. He told me, "It's not good. I've got lung cancer. It is pretty bad, too. I guess 68 years will have to be a long enough life." I let him talk until he seemed to be through. We talked about keeping some hope and about some treatment options.

Then we spent the next half hour talking about hunting and fishing. He had always wanted to go moose hunting. Also, he was an expert fly fisherman at one time, and that sometimes he would just catch the fish and let them go just for the joy of it. Through all of this, even though he was a man with cancer with a rough course ahead, he still was a man with many passions. I am sure I will be seeing more of Hank. It feels good to know that we have started a relationship that will help him feel more at ease when he comes to our unit for treatment.

My next patient was Grace. She was also 68 but looked much, much younger. My first impression was that she was wide-eyed, frightened and pale. She had experienced chest pain the night before that radiated down her left arm. She lived alone, and after a full day's work as a cook in a busy restaurant, she drove herself to the ER in her old pickup truck that had belonged to her husband. My assessments of her were all normal with not a bit of chest pain this a.m. An echocardiogram of her heart was to be done soon and if it was normal, she would go home later that day. The echo proved to be fine and the cardiologist gave her the diagnosis of pericarditis. This is inflammation of the sack around the heart, a benign treatable condition whose cause in many cases, is idiopathic or unknown. The malady usually resolves on its own. It is treated with NSAIDS (nonsteriodal anti-inflammatory drugs such as aspirin, ibuprofen and naproxen) and monitoring. Its symptoms can mimic that of a heart attack. Grace looked so relieved and much calmer when she found out that she would be alright.

I found out a little more about this lady as the day went on. She had lost her husband five years earlier. He had had a heart attack that had begun with symptoms identical to the ones she had experienced the night before. She had performed CPR on her husband until the paramedics arrived, until she was exhausted. Her husband didn't survive. They had been married for 42 years and had 5 children together. She had a son who was an alcoholic and had lost a daughter to cancer. She loved to take her grandson fishing and prided herself in still being able to work full time. When she was finally able to leave, I walked her to the ER door where she had come in the night before to where her old blue truck was parked. She thanked me for taking care of her and went to shake my hand. Instead I reached out and gave her a hug. I was thankful to have gotten to know such a lady. Life had not made her bitter, but stronger.

My third patient Frances was a pleasant 87 year old lady. She was somewhat hard of hearing, which is always a challenge for me as my voice is quiet and hard for older people to hear. She had experienced chest pain the day before while leaving her condo to go shopping down town. This was not a new condition for her so she went ahead and had lunch and shopped. But unfortunately, she had not taken her nitroglycerin pills with her. By the time she had gotten back to the lobby of her condominium, the pain was quite severe. The manager called the paramedics and she was brought to the hospital. She told me how there were lights and sirens everywhere , and she was really quite embarrassed about the whole thing, and if it would have been up to her she just would have just gone up to her condo, taken a nitro, and not made such a fuss about the whole thing. Her assessments were also very stable this morning. The doctor came in and changed some of her medications around a bit and said that if she could walk the approximate distance from the condo to down town without pain, she could also go home. She made twenty laps around the unit at a rapid pace without any problems at all.

I found out that she was separated from her husband of 40 years and was going through a divorce. It seemed a little funny to be divorcing after so many years together and at age 87. She said that there were money issues and ongoing problems with relatives and they were unable to resolve their differences, so they had decided to separate. Her grandson came that afternoon to take this dignified lady back to her home.

And that is how my float day in CCU turned out. It was a smooth and enlightening day in which I cared for a diverse group of patients. And as always, my own life seemed enriched by those that I care for.

A final note:

Hank, my first patient that I took care of that day, spent a great deal of time with us on the cancer unit. He died approximately 2 months after his initial diagnosis from sepsis (a blood infection) and other complications. I was his nurse that final day and was able to hold his hand as he passed away.

Camaraderie

As a nurse, there is a bond, an invisible connection with all other nurses. When you meet another nurse, there is that split second catch of the eyes that says without words, "You know! You know what it is like. You know what it is like to see humanness in its purest form. You have seen it all. You know what it is like to have seen every body fluid imaginable in many different combinations. You know about patients that touch your heart and difficult patients and difficult doctors and having moral issues and ethical issues and all kinds of issues; and having more to do than you possibly have time for and more responsibility than any one person should ever have. You know about being so stressed but having to act calm and together, to portray confidence when you have none, for the sake of the patient and because that is how you are supposed to be. You know about smelling smells so bad that you are almost sick but not letting on; and about trying to find the urethra on a woman when inserting a Foley catheter as perspiration stings your eyes when you would swear that one such orifice does not exist in this person's anatomy. You know about being pushed beyond anything you could imagine. You know about the strength of your character and how it has become that strong because of all that you do, all that you have seen, and all that you have been through. Ah yes, you know!"

Love of My Life

At 5:00 am the music came on reminding me to get up and get ready for work. The bed felt so toasty warm. I looked out the window to see the first snow of the season drifting lightly down. I snuggled over to cuddle in my husband's arms a few more minutes just as Sammy Kershaw began singing *Love of My Life*. "Why couldn't I just stay here for a few more minutes?" I thought.

After stretching things as long as I could, I got in the shower. The warm water felt so good. I dressed and went downstairs to get a bite of breakfast and glance at the paper.

Just as I took a bite of toast, I opened the first page to the obituaries as I had done so many times before. There to my shock was the obituary of a young man we had cared for in the hospital. "Oh no!" I thought. The tears burned and blurred my vision as I tried to read. As I blinked them away I thought, "This isn't fair, right before Christmas!" I thought about his wife and their two small children and what they must be going through. And again, as I do once in a while, I thought, "What keeps me in oncology? This hurts too bad. Why do I keep doing this? Maybe it's time for a change."

Then my mind flashed back to a little over a year earlier. We received a call that Eric, the young man whose obituary I was just reading, was to be admitted to our unit. He had a brain tumor that had been diagnosed some time ago and he had had all the surgical and medical treatment and complications to go along with it.

That day he came to the oncology unit with numerous problems. As Eric was settled in to his bed, there were two of us working to try to gather information, identify problems, carry out doctor's orders and get him stabilized. Eric's wife couldn't find a baby-sitter on such short notice so their little girl was there. Eric's wife was also very pregnant with their second child who would be a little boy.

The little girl who looked to be about 4 years old climbed up on the bed amidst all the commotion as we were starting IVs and giving medications. Oxygen monitors were beeping and alarming. She grabbed her dad's hand and said, "Daddy, what's wrong? Why won't you wake up?" My heart hurt as I told her that her daddy was very sick and we would try to help him to get better but it would take a while. The social workers soon arranged for someone to care for the little girl so her mom could stay at the hospital.

It took two nurses several hours to get Eric stabilized although we were not sure if he was going to make it for a while. Normally, when a patient requires that intensity of nursing care, we have to send them to the intensive care unit but on that day our others patients were doing alright and also our nursing supervisor stepped in to help so we were able to keep Eric with us. He was one of our patients.

He spent several weeks in the hospital and there were a few more times that we almost lost him. But finally right before Christmas, he was able to go home and be with his beautiful family which now included the addition of a new son. A card came from Eric and his wife thanking us for giving them one more Christmas together. We knew it was because of a power greater than anything we had control over.

So as I came back to the present, I thought, this is why I keep doing this, to help someone have one more Christmas, to help them fight the fight even though the battles they win are not as grand as we would hope. I do it because I can and on most days, it gives me great satisfaction even though at times like this morning my strength falters and I need to do some introspection and reevaluation.

And would Sammy Kershaw have sounded so sweet and my husband's arms been so warm and my shower have felt so good if I had not learned the lessons that I had learned from my patients, that each day is a beautiful gift that must be seized and enjoyed and lived to the fullest, because one never knows how many Christmases he has left!

Moments

Nursing can be hard work and very stressful at times. But to me it is about the moments…moments when there is such a connection with another human spirit, and you can feel that you make a difference in another life; by your presence, your knowledge, your insight, and hopefully your wisdom. When you can calm a fear, hold a hand, ease a pain, touch a heart, it is as if your souls are touching. It is why I love doing what I do.

I feel so proud of what I do and that is one of the reasons I wrote this book "One Nurse's Story." I wanted to let people know what nursing is really like, and share some of the moments that I have experienced. Although the details have been changed to maintain patient privacy, the essences of the stories are the same.

I have had the idea to write this book for almost as many years as I have been a nurse. Fears and doubts kept me from writing it. I'm not a writer and…what if I say something I am not supposed to say and what if I make a mistake or hurt someone's feelings or make someone angry? On and on went my doubts. But sometimes bringing something you are passionate about into the world is worth the risk of all those things.

Also too, with the death of my stepfather, I gained some courage. It was almost as if I could hear him saying, "You can tell my story without any fear, and down to the minutest detail. You *need* to tell it. You can tell the humorous parts. You can tell the sad parts. You can tell *my* story because it is *your* story also." I hope you enjoy *Orwin's Story.*

"When you have come to the edge of all
light that you know and are about to drop
off into the darkness of the unknown, faith
is knowing one of two things will happen:
There will be something solid to stand on or
You will be taught to fly"

Patrick Overton

Orwin's Story

How It All Began

I'd been having problems with pain in my leg for five years. Doctors would say you have three crushed disks in your back and that was the reason for the pain. Then I started having kidney stones when we were in Yuma, seven of em in less than a year. I had one so bad I ended up in the hospital. Passin' them suckers hurt! They are sharp!

One of my doctors did an X-ray to see if all the stones were gone. They x-rayed a pretty good sized area. Then I got a call from the doctor. She said, "You have one more kidney stone but you got something a lot worse than that. It showed up on the x-ray that your right femur is fractured." So after fightin' this for five years, the x-ray proved that there really was something wrong.

I was told not to step on that leg anymore because its gonna shatter. Its egg shell thin and it's got three splits in it, so when you step on it, its kinda like a spring and it opens up and when you pick your foot up it closes. It opens up and closes for each step so that is partly why it's painful.

The First Surgery/The Escape

The doctor sent me to surgery and put a rod in my femur to stabilize it. When I got out of surgery they had me on morphine first of all for the pain, and I got pretty goofy. I never have done well on that stuff. So I was off of that and then put on Oxycodone. That didn't go well either so they tried a third medication. I felt pretty OD'd by then, so in the middle of the night the nurses put a thing under the mattress so if I were to get up, it would set off the alarm....but it didn't work too well!

In my mind, I felt like a prisoner. I thought they were going to part me out, you know, take my pieces out, liver and everything, and give whatever to anybody that needed it. I was confused from all of the different combinations of pain meds and was feeling pretty scared! I heard the nurses say something about putting something against the bed so I couldn't get out. That played right into my little screwed up brain.

So I happened to notice my electric wheel chair, brand new at the time, that goes six mile an hour and I figured that if I could get out of that room...well the nurse left the room and I figured I had a little time to get out of that bed...get into that wheel chair and get out of that hospital before they parted me out...because I knew I was next in line.

So I pulled everything out of my veins and got rid of all them tubes and I sneaked real fast over the edge and got out and walked around the stuff and got over to my wheelchair on my leg that had my new rod in it. I just had my hospital gown on and was saturated cuz I'd been sweatin from bein' sceerd. I was soppin wet. I started to go out and then I noticed a head stickin up above the nurses' station which I thought was a guard and, when she looked the other direction, I real quick sneaked out down the hall and got on the elevator. My brain was still all messed up.

So I went down and then I had to go over quite a ways and then all the way down this hall and I'm in my cart, at 6 mile an hour I got er wide open, and nobody in the hall…absolutely nobody and its about 5 o'clock in the morning the first time I went and tried to get out.

I went tearin' down there out through the emergency door and wasn't anybody there, nobody, no guards or anything. So I whizzed out and it was really cold outside and for some reason I thought Marlene, my wife, was gonna be there in a big white Lincoln. So I'm lookin' for a big white Lincoln, goin' up and down the parking lots just as fast as I could go, 6 mile an hour and its freezing and I thought, 'boy I can't handle this cold.' It must have been about 40 degrees out there. It was pretty cold, so I decided I gotta' go back in and get a blanket cuz I was so wet and so cold.

So went right back in where I was and there wasn't anybody in there and this is after 9-11 and anybody coulda went in there and blew the place up; there was no guards, no doctors; nothing. I started going down the hall checking the doors but they'd locked the doors. So I went down probably half a dozen doors, checking them all to see if I could find a blanket and couldn't get in any of them. I happened to look up in the corner and I seen a camera sittin' up there in the ceiling so I thought, 'Oh man if they catch me they'll part me out for sure.'

So I spun that sucker around and I'm getting outta there so I whooped right back out the door and I went across the street and it must have been about 6 am or so by then. They just opened the front gate and people were starting to come in and one lady had seen me as she was coming in, she was one of the nurses there. And so she kind of reported me that this guy shouldn't be runnin around out there with his cart and gown and no clothes on. But I whizzed on out the gate and I got out on 6th Street and I got out to the bus boarding area.

So I whizzed up to the front of the bus, by that time they had the thing all tipped out for me so I got on it. I didn't have a wallet; I didn't have a dime on me, no ID, no nothing and in a hospital gown soppin' wet. They didn't ask me for no money which was nice. I got on the bus and they fastened my wheelchair down after I bumped around in there a few times and wasn't doin' too good. We took off and I was trying to figure out what to do and I still gotta find my wife and by this time I had figured out that she wasn't there.

And then we was just goin' by the Salvation Army on 6th St. so I told the bus driver I needed off. 'I needed off!' Well she went about another 2 blocks before she finally stopped and there wasn't a side walk down there and just sand, and it was pretty steep up to a chain link fence and it was all full of weeds and rocks and what have you, but I got off there anyway and I was goin' down there and kinda worried about my cart tippin' over. I wanted to use their phone so I could call Marlene to come and get me. So I went down through all this trash and bumps and weeds and finally got down to the sidewalk and then made it over to the Salvation Army.

It's a long building and it's got two big doors on it, so I went up to the first one and I looked in the door and I knocked on it and all of a sudden I'm met with this great big guard dog chewin' at the glass on the inside of the door and makin' a big racket and then all of a sudden a guy opened the door and then he put a chain on it so the dog can't shove it open cuz he was tryin' and then he said, "Whatdyawant?!!"

And I said, well, I need to call my wife. Then he said go down to the next door so I whirled around to the next door and I'm freezing to death, and I'm cumin' around a wee bit, but not much.

About that time I heard RRRRAAARRRR (siren) And I thought, oh shoot, I know what that is. I thought what in the world do they want me for?! I'm an adult and I'm on the street but I'm not exactly dressed right. So I just kinda looked straight ahead and I thought maybe they'll just go away but the cop (city police) he says are you the one that escaped from the hospital? And I said yeah I guess that'd be me. And says you gotta go back and I says no I don't. I'm an adult and I don't have to go back. I need to get a hold of my wife. Nope you gotta go back. I argued with him a little bit and there was no arguing with him but he had a kind voice so I went back there. He was a big dude anyway; a policeman. He seen me at the bus stop and was wonderin' why I was sittin' in a bus stop in a gown. He couldn't figure out what in the world is goin' on here and so he says, "We gotta get you back down to the hospital and get this straightened out."

The cop put me inside of the little van (unmarked car) he had. It was cold and he was trying to get the heater to work and it wasn't working and he was trying to get the back double doors open and they wouldn't open. So he called for some assistance and so they sent another car down and he got one of the cops that's been on steroids (you can tell cuz his arms are bigger than his head).

My wheel chair weighs over 300 lbs and he decides he is gonna pick it up and I said you can't pick it up! C'mere and I'll tell you how to run it so you can move it. Well, he's gonna do it his way. I had it set as fast as it could go and it's a joy stick so he grabbed ahold across it while they were tryin to pick it up, they pushed the joy stick, and of course you can't pick up 300 pounds especially if its goin around in circles. And so its spinnin around and he's got one foot in the air and one kinda hoppin along and its spinnin him pretty fast, but then one wheel of the cart (and this cart has big wheels) went over the curb and it's a real high curb. So it just swung the whole thing, him and the machine out in the street and I saw him in one mirror and all of a sudden I seen em in the other mirror. Some how he got loose from it and it stopped and so I guess he figured out he wasn't gonna manhandle this thing.

And so the cop that originally stopped me, he's getting a little upset with the carryin' on there. He got on his radio and says I need someone down here right away with a pickup and a ramp so we can load a big electric wheelchair and I could hear that they were giving him a little static from the other end because they didn't want to be bothered early in the morning and evidently he had a little more seniority than the others because he told them to get that thing down there now and he hung 'er up, and they were down there within a couple of minutes.

They got this old beat up pick up and a ramp which was too narrow. So they kind of got the wheelchair to straddle the thing and they tried to wiggle it back and forth and got it up and when it tipped over into the box it tipped up the ramp and the whole thing and everything went in. I was hopin' they wouldn't trash my new electric wheel chair. It got a few scratches on it but that was all luckily. So they got me down to the hospital and the policemen turned me over to hospital security.

In the meantime they called my wife and they told her "We've lost your husband!" There was about a four second lapse before they said, "But we found him." And in that four seconds my wife thought I had died.

So then they took me right down to X-ray and x-rayed my head because they thought I had something wrong with my head but they x-rayed my leg too. And they took my electric cart away and said they was gonna make a rule that there could be no electric carts in the recovery area. Anyway, that was my escape.

The Second Surgery

I was trying to heal, but my leg still bothered me a lot. I went up to the mayo clinic. It wasn't healing right, they said. They said there still was cancer in the leg and that to get rid of it they might have to cut it straight up and straight out and take my leg and some other stuff off. They said they would do skin graft to keep my insides from comin' out. And I told em I wasn't gonna live like that. I told them that's not the way I live. And I said I'll just go out in the desert and I won't come back cuz I'm not gonna do that and they said, 'Oh don't get all excited.'

There's a guy in Seattle that does marvelous things, and can build people a butt to sit on. Doctors in Coeur d'Alene (CDA) said the same thing. And every doctor we talked to from then on said the same thing. So we went to Seattle and had 'er done and it was quite an operation. But I gotter done and I was in there for 52 days. The surgery lasted for 5 hours.

Right after the surgery I didn't seem to wanna come out of it. I wouldn't wake up. It took a while but I finally came back around and woke up. Family kept talking to me and talking to me and I finally woke up. They didn't know if I was gonna for a while.

I came back to CDA for 3 days. I don't remember much about this. I guess I was delirious because I had an infection.

Now this is important, really important to me. They took me down the Kootenai Hospital and my daughter and son-in-law got me straightened around in there somehow. And I remember when I was coming to, Dr. Brian Samuels gave me some blood and stuff and kinda got my body going.

The nurse asked my wife what I liked for breakfast. And she said I like pancakes and eggs and that sort of thing. I hadn't eaten much while I was in Seattle. But back to CDA; somebody had talked to the dietician so the first thing I remember after wakin' up is pickin' up the top of the little dome that goes over your food and I picked it up a little bit and I saw these half inch thick hot cakes, beautiful! I picked it up a little higher and there's another one on top of that and I picked it up a little higher and there's a great big glazed donut layin' on top a that. And I had two eggs and I had bacon. I thought I must be in heaven. So I licked that platter clean. Things went upward after that.

And I was on the mend from right then. They flew me back to Seattle on the med flight plane because there was some inflammation (infection) there and they had to open me back up and gave me IV antibiotics and I was back home within 3 days. I was on IV antibiotics twice a day for 3 months to clear up the bone infection that I had (osteomylitis). The doctor and his team over there are excellent. They knew what they was doin' and can put somebody's butt back together.

Then they found a spot on my lung last year and thought it was cancer (the chondrosarcoma). After they confirmed that it was, I went back up to see the doctor is Seattle. With my history of Asbestosis, they felt that if they cut the cancer out, I would not get off of the table. That is when I decided to get treatment in Tijuana. I knew it would work cuz it's worked for others. I've got too much too live for now, my wife and kids and grandkids, a new bionic leg and a new shop.

In Tijuana, Mexico we discovered that they have people from all over the world down there. They can help you. They use a lot of vitamin C, and filtering your blood and using oxygen with Ozone in it. They have healed a lot of people down there. We know a guy from Wisconsin that is totally cured.

Orwin's Funny Story

Last time we were there, this was quite a story about Marlene (your Mom). She needed some dental work done and when someone, (me) is in the hospital down there, the dentist gives them a discount. He said he could help her with her teeth, but he needed seven hours or all day to do it. They made her really sleepy, and when he was all done, it was like your mom was drunk, cuz she had been out for seven hours.

She was woogady (couldn't walk straight.) So anyway, I went to get her and my electric wheelchair was parked outside. I was afraid someone was going to steal the little bugger so I was tryin' to keep an eye on it.

I was in there waiting for your mom to take her back to the hotel, and it was way late at night (about 9 or 10 o'clock). All of a sudden we hear this KABOOM! We went outside to see what in the world happened and saw that somebody had thrown a full can of beer at the side of the building. It busted open a little bit and rolled out into the street just outside of where my wheelchair was. Someone ran over the can of beer with their car and when they did, it squirted all over the side of my chair.

So in the meantime the preacher and his wife from the hospital came down there to help us get home. And too…your mom had been there so long that her body kind of relaxed and she had a minor accident you might say. The girl at the dentist office said I don't know exactly how to tell you this, but I think you might want to bring your wife a change of clothes. And so I did.

The preacher and his wife arrived. They said, "We saw your cart out there and we thought we'd help you get your wife back to the hospital." We gets all ready and she's got her wet clothes in a little white plastic bag. The pastor tried to take her bag and your mom says, "No you can't carry that bag." and he says, "Yeah, I'll carry that bag." And she says "Naw, you can't carry that bag!" So I says, "I'll carry that bag." So she gives it to me and I put it on my wheelchair.

And we start out down the street. Well, here's my wife, she's staggerin', and I'm right behind her. The pastor is on one side of her and his wife is on the other. And here I'm cumin' behind with this cart that has just been sprayed with beer and it smelled like we had been out on a real toot and we looked like it too.

So we walked all the way down to the street and back to the hospital and two gals was lookin' at us like somethin' was kind of strange, and I said, "Yeah my wife got drunk and I had to bring her back." Then I said, "Naw, she really didn't she's just been in the dentist's chair for seven hours." I didn't explain to her that I had beer all over and that was an outside job, not an inside job. It really smelled like a brewery.

Then we went up to the room and we were trying to clean the cart up and the pastor was helping and he said we might have to take that down to the car wash tomorrow cuz it's pretty bad.

So they set down on the end of the bed there for a minute and all of a sudden my wife (she was getting new teeth and so they put temporaries in, and one of her temporary teeth that they put in the top front kept poppin' out) wanted to explain about not wantin' the preacher to hold the bag. So she said "I wet my pants!" And about that time, her right top front tooth popped out and landed on the bed!

With all the events of the evening that was more than the pastor could handle. He just busted out laughin'. He couldn't even sit up any more. He just laid back on the bed and just laughing like a bugger and every time he would think of it he would start laughin' again. Anyway things happen!

The Pastor was cured of cancer at this same hospital and now he is working here helping others get through what he went through. Everything is happy. They are a bunch of angels. They just build you up and give you hope!

Mom's Story

A Christmas letter, December 2007

Dear Friends and Relatives,

It's been another year of ups and downs since doctors told us Orwin had six months to live. That was March 15th 2007 after a biopsy of the lung to identify the kind of cancer it is—chondrosarcoma, the same kind that took his leg and is inoperable. They said they "would keep him comfortable till the end."

So our journey continues with Alternative Medicine in Tijuana Mexico. The medical team there at least gave us HOPE. One has to have hope.

People from all over the world go there to try and beat their cancers. We met a lady from Saudi Arabia. She was very ill and had four small boys at home. Other places, Denmark, Spain, England, South Africa, Norway, New York, Wisconsin, Texas and Seattle just to name a few.

They treat the mind and spirit in addition to treating Orwin using different kinds of medications. I went to classes to learn cooking healthy and learned to give him his shots. Positive thinking and laughing, relaxation, prayer and worship classes for both of us. He is also on a small dose of chemo drug.

….We have made it past 6 months. Every day is a blessing from God.

Love,
Marlene

My Story

September 21, 2008

Dear Orwin,

No one could have told your story as well as you, so I left it mostly in your words. (Edited for clarity) It is poignant, genuine and at times very humorous. And as you turn 70 years old today, I want to tell you what an incredible person you are!

I will never forget the day of your surgery when they took your leg. I had to work that day and I could hardly concentrate thinking about what you were going through. Even though I knew it was to save your life, I couldn't imagine how it would be for you to go into surgery with two legs and come out with only one. And then when we got the phone call that you weren't waking up; the tears just came and I couldn't stop them. I was so relieved when we finally heard that the surgery went well and it wasn't as extensive as it could have been and that you were finally waking up. And you were so brave going through such a tremendously long recovery...52 days!

I remember the day after you came home. I think the reality set in for you that your leg was gone and to see you shake with sobs and hear you say that you wouldn't have gone through this if it wasn't for all of us kids. It truly broke my heart, even though I know those tears were probably necessary to begin the healing process from all that you had gone through.

You have fought such a courageous battle and have done it with dignity and perseverance and I believe you are winning the battle. A few months ago I saw you up on a ladder wearing your new artificial leg putting up a light fixture. I thought it was one of the workmen working on the shop but was so surprised to see that it was you. I do not know of any other person dealing with what you are dealing with who is doing as well as you are and with such strength and bravery.

Another extremely special memory I have is on my 50th birthday. I wanted to do something daring and memorable to jump into the second half of my life, so I decided to go sky diving, but I didn't know how scary it would be going up over twelve thousand feet in the air and jumping out of an airplane. You were there to watch. But you sensed my escalating fear and said, "I'll go up with you and jump too so you won't be so sceered." So we trained together that day and both did a tandem jump from that airplane, you going first and me right after you, and you with your one leg! It is a day I will never forget!

To see Orwin's original skydiving video go to www.youtube.com and search *Orwin Skydiving* and watch part one and part two.

Or, type in your browser

http://www.youtube.com/watch?v=vS-VSR_EtRk

and

http://www.youtube.com/watch?v=FIXXyf75CHU&feature=mfu_in_order&list=UL

I want to thank you for accepting me and my family as your own. You are a gentle and loving father figure that I look up to greatly. Thank you for all you have done for me over the years. I am very proud to have you as a step dad and also very proud of the kind of man you are.

Love Delraya

October 2009

Orwin is coming upon his 5 year mark surviving sarcoma. He just had a third surgery in which a wedge was taken from his left lung to remove two sarcoma nodules. He also had one lobe of his right lung removed to get rid of seven nodules; so his battle continues. Recently after returning to their winter home in Yuma, he spent a night in the hospital due to a fever of 104 degrees. He had pneumonia along with a urinary tract infection, but has recovered from both. We don't know exactly what the future holds, but we know that Orwin will continue fighting with everything he's got.

December 2009

Orwin had been having trouble with pain in his jaw. A biopsy revealed chondrosarcoma. An MRI of the brain showed spots of unknown origin. Orwin has been having trouble thinking and also with his balance. There is talk of doing biopsies of the brain and more surgeries to remove the lesions if they are sarcoma. That is what he wants to do...continue the battle. We are thinking "How much more can he take and also how much more can Mom take?" The decision on what to do next was decided for us, *as it always is*. Orwin is slipping away a little more each day. No additional surgeries will help. It is time to stop fighting.

February 14, 2010 ♥

Dear Orwin,

You are loved so much by so many! It is hard to watch you slip slowly away from us. You fought the battle so valiantly. Thank you for embracing us as if we were your own.

Love,

Delraya, Rich, Christie, Mike,
Braden, Brock, Bryce, Kevin, Jeff,
Heidi, Mercadies, and Ry Ry

Saying Goodbye.

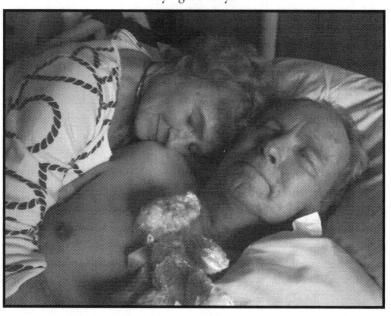

February 20, 2010

Memories of Last Night with Orwin.

We have all been keeping vigil here at the Hospice house watching over you. Mom has been here the most but she needed some rest. I think she knew tonight was the night because in her exhausted state, she said her last goodbye before leaving to get some sleep.

We wanted someone to always be with you. I am laying here on the fold out bed in your room listening to you breathe...and not breathe. We all know it is getting close. The periods of apnea are lasting 35 seconds. No matter how many times I have seen this, and how much I know the process, I am not prepared to watch a loved one die.

Cindy is at your side. I grabbed a pillow and blanket and went out on the couch by the fireplace to give her some time alone with her dad. It has been a long broken up night. The next thing I am aware of is someone talking to me. "Your Dad's breathing has changed a great deal. We just repositioned him. I think it is getting close," I heard the nursing assistant say to me. I felt like an electric shock was sent through me as I bounded up, and headed the few feet to his room.

The scene that I met was much the same as before but Cindy was gently sobbing and Orwin's breath's had stopped. "Is he gone?" I said, and through tears she shook her head, "Yes."

His six-year battle with sarcoma had ended a 6 am on February 20, 2010. When I was a nurse in the hospital, we would talk about how you could always tell what kind of life a person lived by the energy left in the room when they departed from this physical realm. I even put my head up and my arms out to capture the feeling as you would during a warm rain. I *felt* as I stood in the peace that was present in the room, what I already *knew*, that he had lived a good life and was headed toward a good place.

We found out later that right about that time his son Dave had a dream in which his Dad told him that he was leaving and that it was ok.

I can picture him free, free of the phantom pain, and working on his tractors with both legs! One might want to think that Orwin lost his battle with Sarcoma because it took his life, I would say that he is such a winner! We all have our battles and the final outcome is the same for all of us. But how we fight our personal struggles is what makes us successful. Continuing to embrace and love life, hope and persevere makes you a successful hero in my book. I am going to miss you.

Love,
Delraya

Orwin Orval Evenson

Born in New Deal, Montana on Sep. 21, 1938

Departed on Feb. 20, 2010 and resided in Dalton Gardens, ID.

Visitation: Friday, Feb. 26, 2010
Funeral Service: Friday, Feb. 26, 2010
Cemetery: Coeur d' Alene Memorial Gardens

Orwin Orval Evenson's six year battle with sarcoma ended, Saturday, February 20, 2010, as he passed away peacefully at age 71. He was born on September 21, 1938 in New Deal, Montana to Orval and Fay Evenson. He was the second oldest in a family  of six children, Dorothy, Karen, Janice, Kenneth and Eileen. He is survived by his wife of 25 years, Marlene Evenson . Together they lovingly blended their families; his daughters, Kathy Triggs (Richard), Cindi Koller (Greg) and son, Dave Evenson by his first marriage to Margaret (Campbell) Woodward and Marlene's daughters; Delraya Anstine (Rich) and Tammy Baker (Larry) and their 14 grandchildren, Mathew, Nathan, Melissa, Emily, Zachary, Nicholas, Garren, Samantha, Maygen, Garrett, Christie, Jeff, Angela, Chris and also 5 great grandchildren, Braden, Brock, Bryce, Mercadies and Rylan.

As a young man Orwin spent 5 years in the Navy on the USS Staten Island. Setting up Little America in the South Pole, banding 500 empire penguins and participating in Operation Deepfreeze II were among some of his most memorable accomplishments. This time frame also began his 45 year career in refrigeration as he learned how to maintain the ships boilers and refrigeration systems.

After holding jobs with Buttrey's and Market Equipment, he was able to open his own business, Orwin's Arctic Refrigeration in Dalton Gardens, Idaho. After retirement, he and Marlene enjoyed hunting, fishing, traveling to and from their home in Yuma, Arizona and spending time with family and friends.

His battle with cancer took his leg. But he kept on going and inspired others in so many ways. In spite of his disability he still worked on his many tractors and even went skydiving.

Orwin's kind and generous spirit touched many, from those near and dear, to strangers in need. He loved to tell stories, especially about growing up on the farm in Montana. His generous heart will be missed by all.

Obituary written by Tammy Baker

Tribute to Orwin

It is interesting how after someone dies, the world just keeps turning. Earthquakes occur, husbands go fishing, colds happen, assignments still have due dates...doesn't the world know that it should just stop, out of respect, just for a little bit? The sun shouldn't come over the mountain, the moon shouldn't shine so brilliantly, the bobsledders shouldn't be speeding down the track at 96 miles per hour and figure skaters shouldn't perform on the ice...although maybe... as I watched the poignant performance of Joannie Rochette only three days after her mother died of a sudden heart attack, things are exactly as they should be. Afterwards, through tears and with her hand on her heart, she mouthed a message to her mother in French. I'm not sure what she said, maybe "I love you," or "this was for you Mom." So Orwin, as in your life, you showed us how to live, our lives will go on, and I promise to live as richly and passionately as possible, embracing all the wonders of this wonderful world....that is my tribute to you.

Love always,
Delraya

"When you have come to the edge of all light that you know and are about to drop off into the darkness of the unknown, Faith is knowing One of two things will happen: There will be something solid to stand on or You will be taught to fly"

We will miss you Orwin!

Still Here

You looked at me and saw what I never could see
You made me feel more than I thought I could ever be
...you were always there to lift me up, to make me strong
You're not gone ...You're still here in my heart...

Song by Natasha Bedingfield

My Most Irrational Thought

This is the second time I almost quit nursing school. It happened right before Christmas toward the end of my first semester. We were just beginning our OB/GYN rotation (Obstetrics and Gynecology), new babies and new mothers! I was not adverse to massaging funduses and palpating breasts and helping new mothers with their personal needs. I had been through it myself twice. But the newborns scared me to death! I was so afraid that I would do something wrong or miss something on my assessment and cause harm to someone's neonate. As I read through the six hundred fifty pages of my *Essentials of Maternal-Newborn Nursing*, there were twelve pages in very small print relating to the neonatal assessment, the normal findings and alterations in normal findings and possible causes. The assessments were so different in these wee ones compared to an adult. We had been taught over and over again in nursing school to always consider the very young and the very old in a unique way as they are so susceptible to things that most humans can adjust to easily.

As I read that low blood pressure could be due to hypovolemia or low fluid volume and could cause shock and that a weak pulse could be caused be decreased cardiac output and bradycardia or slow pulse could be an indication of severe asphyxia and elevated temperature could mean sepsis or brain damage, and on and on for twelve pages, my stress level was so high it was almost debilitating.

Also, the semester went right up until just a short time before Christmas. With finals approaching in addition to preparing for hospital clinical, everything seemed to be so intense and taking all my time. With holiday music and decorations all around and two small children, I just wanted to stop and be able to enjoy the season, enjoy my family, enjoy my life, clean my house, and watch "It's A Wonder Life"!

I had taken time out that I didn't really have one evening to make Christmas cookies for my daughter's Christmas party the next day. Normally I would have enjoyed the whole process, but my whole life seemed to be one big stress. How can I stop this insanity and save face? As I added the ingredients into my big super-powered Kitchen Aid mixer, I watched the beater go round and round slowly at first and then faster and faster. Hmm.....What if I......just stick my hand right in that mixer...what would it do!? Possibly break a couple of fingers. But then I would have to drop out of nursing school. I would have to. Then I could live again and enjoy my family and the season, enjoy my life. I could always go back to school again, later.

Luckily I didn't stick my hand in the mixer. But I did make an appointment to talk to my advisor that next day about thoughts about wanting to quit. As we talked she said that she couldn't make that decision for me but that she knew I could get through it and that the semester would be over soon, and there would be a break and time to rejuvenate. She eased my mind, too, about neonatal care. She said I would not be out there solely on my own, and that as long as I knew my assessments and was prepared for clinical I would get through it. And she was right.

I've told that story a few times since then to other nurses and it is always met with laughter and most of them saying that they understood. One nurse said that she had wanted to get in a car accident when she was a student.

A great friend and wonderful certified nurse's assistant at the Cancer Center entered nursing school recently and toward the end of the first semester she was stressed to the max, had lost 25 pounds from worry and was struggling with finals and was ready to quit. I received an E-mail from Kimmy saying that she was just about to put her hand in the mixer. I guess I must have told her that story too. Following is a letter from Kimmy as she leaves us to continue her education.

Goodbye-I'll Miss You Guys

Thank you for the goodbye party, cake, and hugs.

As many of you know I have been here at the Cancer Center for eight years and at Kootenai Medical Center for ten and a half years. I leave reluctantly, but know that it will be best for my family and education. Many of you here have seen me through so much of my life that you have been like family to me. You have seen me through getting back together with Kelly, my husband. We will celebrate fifteen years, minus the three years we had to separate and grow up.

You've been there through Ethan's diagnosis of Autism, and helped me keep going when I felt I didn't have the strength. Ethan will start regular kindergarten next year, and is on his way to a typical first grade classroom. Yay, for miracles!

You have held me when I cried because I had thyroid cancer and supported me through my time off and recovery. We celebrated together when I got into the nursing program (my ten-year, two-year degree). You cheered me on through my thirtieth birthday in August, and helped carry me through the nursing program until I was strong enough to walk on my own two feet.

There are so many memories I will cherish with so many of you. I know that if there is anything I ever need I will know where I can come for help and support from friends.

It has been an honor and a privilege to work with all of you. I will miss you all very much.

Love, Kimmy

Footnote: As Kimmy (Kim) begins her second year of nursing school, her goals are far-reaching. I know she will achieve them all. It has been like watching my own child grow up. What an incredible young lady, intelligent and with insight beyond her years. She has wonderful things to offer the world and some day after we have all retired....she might be running this place!

2nd Footnote: The forward in this book is from Kimmy. She has been working in her RN role on night shift on the oncology unit for a couple of years now. I can only imagine how blessed her patients are to have her caring for them. The story, *A God Thing*, is also written by her.

Three Nurse Angels

January 9, 2006 was not to be a routine day at work but a day that I would remember forever.

I was working with Dr. Tezcan that day. The nurse that is normally with him was ill. I am the fill in, or float nurse. It is what I love to do most. I feel like a hero, helping out when needed, and I slide easily into most positions.

It began when my step-mom showed up that morning at our clinic to say that they had found my grandmother unconscious beside her bed, and the ambulance had brought her into the emergency room. Her health had been deteriorating over the past few months, but family members had done everything they could to keep her in her own home. She was 94, and up until six months prior, she was active and mentally sharp.

She was just a little lady with a Norwegian heritage, but had so much pride and spunk, and had been on her own since losing my grandfather almost 20 years before. She never liked visiting doctors, never had checkups, wasn't on any medications, and had never had a pap smear or a mammogram. She had done her own yard work and maintained a meticulously manicured lawn, with a succulent vegetable garden, and floral display for which she earned many community accolades.

Picture from local newspaper August 1970

She taught my sister and I how to make lefsa many years before, a tradition I have continued, making it for my own family and friends, and even making into a small business around the holidays She told us, "Now I don't tell this to many people, but if you put a pinch of sugar in the potatoes as you mash them, your lefsa will be nice and golden brown."

Today the news from the doctor was daunting. She probably would not be alive more than three more days. They had admitted her to the hospital to one of the circle-of-life rooms on the oncology unit which is set aside for dying patients.

My mind rushed to come up with a plan. Should I try to go now? We were having a very busy day and also there was no one to take my place. There was no way I could go then...but maybe in a little while. The doctor had said three days hadn't he? I could wait a little longer.

Things never did slow down at work, and in talking to family members, it seemed that Grandma Kay was not getting any worse, so I just decided to go across the street to the hospital when I had finished for the day. I was just finishing up my day when the call came from my husband. "I'm sorry Babe but your Grandma just passed away."

Tears came. Normally I can control them, but not right now. I was sad that I didn't get to say goodbye, and mad that I hadn't found a way to leave sooner. And for me sad plus mad equal lots of tears.

Mary Lee, one of the nurses that I work with and also a very dear friend took me into one of the empty patient exam rooms. She had lost her mother not long before. She was a great support and comfort to me. *She was my first angel.*

I had always felt so bad when family and friends didn't get to say goodbye to a loved one, but now I knew myself what it felt like. Also, I am an oncology nurse and I know that death is something that we all must face, and I don't have difficulty being with someone as they die. I should have been there with her holding her hand.

When I had control of my emotions, I took the underground tunnel to the hospital to the oncology unit where Grandma was. I had worked on this unit for 13 years before coming to the outpatient clinic seven years earlier. Upon arriving there, I saw many familiar faces. I told them why I was there. They were all so concerned and so sorry. If they had known that she was my grandmother, they all said, they would have called when she was getting close to dying.

I was directed to the room where Grandma was. I entered and saw her laying there with her hands folded. The look of serenity on her face was a look I had never seen before, nor did I see this genuineness of her true quintessence at the funeral. She was glowing and so serene as she passed from this life into the next. I wanted to look up toward the ceiling to see what she had seen, but I guessed I already knew.

One of the nurses, Val, entered the room. Having worked with her before, and for so many years, I always had admired the kind of nurse she was, always so full of compassion. She hugged me and stayed with me and shed tears with me. *That was my encounter with my second angel.*

Then my husband arrived. He too commented on how peaceful Grandma looked. We sat there in the stillness for quite awhile.

When it was time to leave, Linda came up to me and said that she had been my grandmother's nurse, and also apologized for not getting in touch with me. She is a float pool nurse, meaning that she goes to different areas of the hospital when needed, just like myself. I also had worked side by side with her over the years with great admiration. She said that relatives had been there all day, but had gone to eat dinner. Linda had been in Grandma's room and while it was quiet, when it was just the two of them, she could tell that she was dying. She sat and held my grandma's hand and prayed as Grandma Kay breathed her last breath. Linda said "I don't know if your Grandma was a believer, but I prayed." *Thank you Linda, you are not just a wonderful nurse, but the third angel that I encountered that day.*

Then I realized that things had happened just as they were supposed to. My Grandmother was a proud and private person. She waited until everyone was gone before leaving the world. If I had been there, she wouldn't have let go. She was going to do it on *her* time and only when *she* was good and ready, and that is exactly what she did!

I miss you Grandma. I miss your stories and hearing you say "Oofta!" I miss walking around your yard seeing the beautiful flowers and smelling the wonderful fragrances, the taste of fresh peas from your garden…and so many other things. I will always hold those memories dear in my heart.

It has now been over five and a half years since my grandmother passed away, and today I received this story written by my last nurse angel. I had no idea she had written it until now. This is her perception of that day. I am still so grateful for what she did then, and in awe of how our lives are all intertwined.

Linda's Story

My story is not one of great heroics or excitement, but is very meaningful to me. I was called in to float to the oncology department, and one of the Circle of Life patients was very close to passing just as I was coming on shift. The family was notified and they were not able to make it in.

Not wanting the patient to die alone, I sat with her and held her hand. Although she was comatose, I talked to her, prayed for her and it was not long before this frail elderly lady took her last breath.

The family was notified that she had passed and within fifteen minutes her granddaughter arrived. She stood there with tears in her eyes and said she wished she would have known, she was just across the street working at the cancer center. This was one of my co-workers, who worked on this unit years ago.

I stood there with tears in my eyes and a lump in my throat, thinking of her not being with her grandmother when she passed. Then my co-worker committed the greatest act of compassion, with tears in her eyes she gave me a hug and thanked me for not letting her die alone, said her grandmother was a Christian and knows she appreciated the prayers.

She made me feel honored to be with her grandmother as she slipped out of this life and stepped into the next.

I think of this story often when taking care of patients. *Every patient is somebody's loved one.*

Linda Lamon RN
(My third Nurse Angel)

Jim

This is a poem written by a patient while he was getting a blood transfusion one day. Jim was a wonderful man who was my husband's boss at one time. He was always friendly and cheerful and full of good spirit even toward the end. He wrote us poems most every day he was with us.

I was down at the center getting blood and laying on my back
The only thing I could see on ceiling was the long old curtain track

Once in a while a big black spider would
show up on the ceiling above
He even came down on his web and told me of his love

He said Jim, I have this sweet young thing
up there with a red spot on her back
She is up there on our nest that is just
behind the first bend in the track

I have to go now Jim to answer her beck and call
He went on home to see her, you want to know what happened
SHE ATE HIM guts feathers and all

The moral of this story is

If you have a lover with a red spot on her back
Get the hell out of there and never look back.

Philanthropy

The dictionary defines philanthropy as the effort to increase the well-being of human-kind through charitable donations intended to promote human welfare.

I have always wanted to be a philanthropist. I love the word, how it rolls off my tongue and I love the thought of donating to make a difference. Although I do what I can now, if I had great sums of money, I would donate to causes that resonate within me; give more to the Fistula Foundation in Ethiopia for Dr.Catherine Hamlin's organization to return dignity to young women whose lives are shattered by giving birth when their bodies aren't ready; sponsor more children through World Vision; donate to help find a cure for sarcoma that took my step-father's right leg and two lobes of his lungs and ultimately his life; and donate to help find answers about Restless Leg Syndrome that has plagued my husband for years.

But it is not always monetarily that we can be great givers. My husband donates a part of himself approximately twice a month. He is a platelet donor. He has donated almost 300 times. And being a big man, he is often able to give a double and even triple batch.

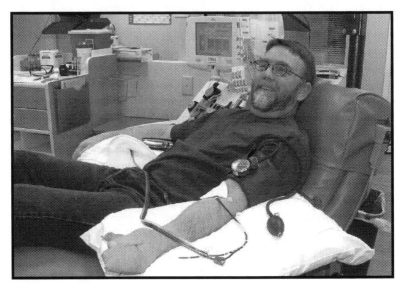

Photo by Kerri Rankin Thoreson

As an oncology nurse, I know how blood and platelet transfusions are life-renewing for patients whose treatments lower their blood counts. Chemotherapy kills the rapidly growing cancer cells, but some good cells are also affected, such as platelets and other cells in the body. Often we need to support people through the low times with transfusions until their bone marrow is able to catch up with the demand. Also, we treat many older people whose bone marrow just seems to get "tired" and no longer makes the right amount or the right kind of blood cells. This is called MDS or Myelodysplastic Syndrome. These people's lives can be enriched and extended through the transfusions that they receive. These are only a few of the reasons people may need platelets.

Blood platelets keep a person from bleeding. A person's normal platelet count is between 140,000 and 440,000 microliters of blood, which is a very small amount. Patients who need transfusions get down to 7,000 or below. They can get nose bleeds, bleeding gums if they brush their teeth too vigorously, bruising with the slightest bump and petechiae (another of my favorite words), which are little tiny red dots that are pinpoint hemorrhages the people may see on their arms, legs or trunk when they do not have enough platelets.

They are the most numerous of the three types of blood cells but are also the smallest and the lightest. Under a microscope they look like a red tire with a transparent center. When there is a tear in a blood vessel, the platelets begin to change shape and grow tentacle like structures that reach out and make contact with the broken blood vessel wall and also other platelets. This forms a plug that seals the area of trauma so that bleeding stops. This is a very simplified version but it gives one an idea of how these amazing guys do their job.

There are random donor platelets which are taken from many different units of blood already donated, and single donor platelets (also called apheresis platelets) taken from one person. This is what my husband does.

Small amounts of his blood are removed and the platelets are centrifuged or spun out and the red cells are reinfused while he lays with a large needle the size of a small straw it seems, in his anticubital space, which is the place where most people get routine blood drawn from the inside of the elbow. The whole process takes about two to three hours. These single donor platelets are what we always order for our cancer patients because with already weakened immune systems from both the cancer and their treatment, it is much easier for their bodies to accept these.

Monetarily, with each unit being around $700.00 and being able to give double and triple batches, that adds up to around a quarter to a half of a million dollars. Time wise this is around 600 plus hours sitting in a chair with a needle in his arm. Also with his Restless Leg Syndrome, this is no easy feat.

So as I regulate the rate on the tubing and watch the thick cloudy yellow fluid slowly drip into my patient and I see that the platelets are from the O Positive blood group and I know that he has donated within the last 5 days, I wonder. Could they possibly have once belonged to my husband? But if so, they have a new home and a new job to do, possibly to help keep an individual on course for their next chemotherapy treatment, to boost an elderly person's platelet count when their own bone marrow is too worn out to make platelets, or keep someone from bleeding from so many sources and just possibly saving a life.

I am so proud of you honey. You are a philanthropist of the purist kind.

Photo by Kerri Rankin Thoreson

Conquering Cancer

When one comes in for their first chemotherapy treatment, he or she always has a deer in the headlight, terrified gaze. After the shocking diagnosis of cancer, the thought of piercing needles and chemicals being pumped into their body is just about as bad. All the education and all the literature in the world cannot prepare them for this first treatment.

But it is only after their IV line is in place and their questions answered, that they begin to settle into their recliner a bit. With their head on a soft pillow and covered by a blanket fresh from the warmer, they notice all the commotion around them.

One lady asks when she will be done because she has an appointment to have her nails done in a half hour; another patient who is a school teacher is working on lesson plans for her students. Another is crocheting and a gentleman is watching Fox News. A nurse needs to hang a chemotherapy bag for one of her patients but he isn't in his chair. She finally finds him at the other end of the room, IV and all, visiting with a friend he has met at the clinic who is also getting treatment. People are exchanging recipes and talking about their Harley rides, doing Sudoku and talking on cell phones.

Your patient looks at you and says, "Are all these people getting chemo?" You say, "Most of them, yes." He looks relieved as if to say, "Maybe I can do this too and it won't be so bad." And you know that after a couple of times, this person, too, will be joining all the others and looking at their chemotherapy as an uninvited part of their day but not so terribly unpleasant.

It is an exciting time to be an oncology nurse. I have seen such tremendous progress over my 23 years as a nurse. Great strides are being made in treatments, new drugs emerging constantly and outcomes improving. It seems that if one drug won't work, the doctor always has another endeavor. Although some people are very ill, many manage quite well. And even if it can't be cured, in many cases cancer can be treated like a chronic illness just like diabetes or heart and lung problems.

Although we still have battles to fight, we are victorious in so many ways. We are closer to conquering cancer than ever before.

A Bit of a Miracle

I was visiting with a kind older gentleman about seven years ago who had come into the outpatient clinic for treatment. As I talked with him while starting his IV, I found that he had lived in our town all his life just like myself. Instead of the usual things that I say, such as talking about what the town used to be like, for some reason blurted out that my grandmother had lived at 1111 Front St. I have never done that before and have never done it since, but on this particular day, that is the way I took the conversation. This was my wonderful grandmother who passed away from endometrial cancer on December 5th 1976, around 25 years earlier; my Grandma Celeste that I spoke of in the introduction that had been such an encouragement to me in my life.

The patient then said to me "I grew up in that house." I thought he was kidding at first but then I realized he was very serious. I said, "You mean you lived in my grandma's house!?" He then said "No, that is not exactly right. She lived in *my* house."

As we sat and reminisced about all the features of the home such as the cut glass window in the parlor, I could almost see my grandmother sitting at her piano. She would sing and play dance hall tunes from her younger days and teach us songs like *Three Blind Mice, Chop Sticks* and *Smokey the Bear*. We remembered the wood stove in the kitchen. Grandma sometimes still used it for cooking, but mostly for heat. I can still smell the wood scent of the presto logs that she used. There was the creaky staircase that led up to the many bedrooms. I don't think it was so creaky when my patient that day had lived there, probably because of my sister and I and all the cousins sliding down the banister over and over.

We talked about the big covered porch that spanned the whole front of the house. As little girls, my sister and cousins and I would play dress up there in old dresses, hats, high-heeled shoes and such, that still had the fragrance of the old trunk that they were stored in. Then we would parade up and down the sidewalk in front of the house with our baby buggies and baby dolls. The sidewalk was cracked and heaved up from tree roots. Not bad for baby buggies but if you were on your roller skates, those bumps could send you flying. Those few minutes took me back to some wonderful times in my young life.

The patient died a very short time after our visit that day. I mentioned to my mother that I had met the man that lived at one time at 1111 Front and that he had passed away. She said that my grandmother had probably wanted to know how things were going for us down here. He could tell her that her loved ones were doing well once he got to heaven. I am not sure about that, but I know the fates were truly aligned, and I experienced a bit of a miracle that day…the day I met the man that lived in my grandmother's house.

"There are only two ways to live your life.

One is as though nothing is a miracle.

The other is as though everything is a miracle."

- Albert Einstein

The following poem was given to me by a very brave man toward the end of his life while he was getting blood transfusions. He couldn't see and could barely walk but after reading this poem I know that his life was very rich in all the ways that counted. I have his permission and blessing to share it with others.

The Quest

In my youth I sought recognition in all things.

*I sought recognition for my robust health and
energy and found I was only ordinary.*

*I sought recognition for wit and cleverness and
found the folly and poverty of my mind.*

*I sought recognition in illuminating the frailty and weakness
of others and found only the infirmity of my own character.*

*I sought recognition in knowledge and conversation
that I might be wiser and more learned than most in all
matters. I found this boring to myself and others.*

*I sought recognition for my possessions and importance and
found only vanity, deception, and loneliness in my pursuit.*

*I sought recognition for light verse and prose only to
find the domain reserved for the gifted. I agonized
over shattered dreams and disappointments.*

*In my quest for recognition I found a quiet
desperation and knew the malady within.*

*Therein I searched for recognition and found truth—a truth that
rang through every crevice and recess of my mind and heart:*

Know Thy God and Be Thyself.
I searched no more.

(Neal W. Roberson)

So You Had a Bad Day

A bad day at the Cancer Center happens rarely. But here is one that I didn't go so good.

I was scheduled as the float nurse. Normally I love this position. My job is to do whatever needs to be done to help the clinic run smoothly. I like feeling helpful, and usually everyone is so appreciative of all that I do for them. This float day *felt* a bit different though.

It started with our monthly nursing meeting for which I showed up a half hour late because I had forgotten. When I walked in, I heard lots of people stating their cases, lots of blame, lots of loud voices and people talking at the same time. Some topics were emerging that I hadn't heard about for awhile. The BUDGET!

Census is a bit down...More overtime...Why can't nurses get out on time! And again that authoritative tone of voice that I hate so much is everywhere. We need to take responsibility; need to plan our day better; turn over our assignments to other nurses staying late so we can get out on time. I begin to hear Charlie Brown's teacher's voice. Waah Waah Waah Waah! Funny thing is before I came to the meeting, I thought we were all doing a great job. I am wishing that I had missed the second half of the meeting instead of the first which was a half hour presentation on sexuality and dealing with cancer. Now that would have been worthwhile. I think the meeting set the tone for the whole clinic that day because everyone seemed picky, crabby and uptight.

After the meeting I was asked to take over for one of the doctor's nurses for a short time. I was to meet with a patient coming into our clinic for the first time and present the patient information to the physician. She was an elderly lady and very hard of hearing and did not have an accurate medication list with her, but instead had brought all of her medication bottles to the clinic in a bag about the size of Santa's pack. It took quite a while to sort through the meds and figure out what she was and wasn't taking. The fact that she was very hard of hearing didn't help matters much.

It took quite a while to do this and gather all of the other information I needed to get. By the time I met with the doctor, I could see he was frustrated that he didn't have his regular nurse and angry because I had taken so long and put him behind.

After that, one of the nursing assistants decided to plan my day for me by telling me which patients I needed to see and that I should go upstairs and get some pain medication for another patient. Again there was that authoritative voice. I took a deep breath and tried to calm down for about fifteen minutes then called the nursing assistant over to talk with her in private. "Please don't tell me what I *need* to do. If you want to make a suggestion, I will listen but then it is up to me to decide what to do." I said. "OK OK. I will try to do better," she stammered.

My next job was to go to the chemotherapy suite to cover a nurse's assignment while she met with our manager. When she gave me report on what needed to be done, I was overwhelmed. A patient is here for first treatment and needed blood drawn from his central line catheter…and there is a problem with drug approval from the insurance company and I might want to call social services to check on that… a patient needs a chemotherapy push (which is a process that involves about 15 minutes of one-on-one time with him)…and another patient's blood transfusion will be done soon…take his IV out and let him go home…the patient in the bed is having nausea and vomiting. Watch for his chart from the doctor with orders for fluids and antinausea medications…the next scheduled patient had just arrived and needs an IV started…and on and on went the instructions.

I said to the nurse that maybe this wasn't the best time for her to be leaving and maybe she should get things a little more under control before she left. The charge nurse that day overheard the conversation and agreed that that was a lot to be leaving for me to do, but she said she would help. Both of us worked the whole time the nurse was gone to get her caught up. When the nurse came back, she did apologize for leaving me with so many lose ends.

I arrived home that evening and was sitting on the deck venting to my husband about my day. He listened intently and added supportive nods at just the right time. I was feeling better already. And then he said, "I am sorry you had a bad day, but do you know what? We're going fishing?" I said, "I'll go change."

We take our little boat out on pristine Hayden Lake, and have the whole lake to ourselves and it is a gorgeous evening. I sit in the bow of the boat, the wind blowing through my hair. While we glide across the smooth water, the cares of the day are also whisked away. The fish are biting and the catching is good. As dusk sets in, a full moon peaks up over the mountains and I have such admiration for all the beauty around me. I feel grateful and loved, and I know… tomorrow will be a better day!

Promise Yourself

To be so strong that nothing can disturb your peace of mind.

To talk health, happiness, and prosperity
to every person you meet.

To make all your friends feel that there is
something worthwhile in them.

To look at the sunny side of everything and
make your optimism come true.

To think only of the best, to work only for the
best and to expect only the best.

To be just as enthusiastic about the success
of others as you are about your own.

To forget the mistakes of the past and press on
to the greater achievements of the future.

To wear a cheerful expression at all times and give
a smile to every living creature you meet.

To give so much time to improving yourself that
you have no time to criticize others.

To be too large for worry, too noble for anger, too strong for
fear, and too happy to permit the presence of trouble.

To think well of yourself and to proclaim this fact to
the world, not in loud word, but in great deeds.

To live in the faith that the whole world is on your side,
so long as you are true to the best that is in you.

Christian D. Larson

Glimpses

When I look back on my many years of nursing, I see flashes of people, conversations and experiences.

-Of being a brand new nurse working the night shift when a confused little old lady came running out of her room stark naked holding her bloody IV catheter in her hand that she had just pulled out and dragging the tubing and bag behind her. She was headed right toward me as I thought," What in the world have I gotten myself into!"

-Of working the night shift and a group of nurses standing together visiting in the med room about 4:00 am talking about the sleep we had gotten the previous days before. We were all sleep deprived and were intrigued by stories and envious of other coworkers who had slept for six hours straight without waking up or had gotten a two hour nap before coming to work. We were like a bunch of people on diets standing around talking about food.

-A young gentleman fighting leukemia that had been in isolation and confined to his room for several weeks. His white count had reached a safe level and his temperature remained normal after weeks of fevers and having to have ice baths. He slipped on some now baggy Levis for the first time in many weeks and began sobbing at the pure joy of being out of his room and being able to walk down the hall.

-Of caring for a woman with a terminal condition but with an unquenchable sense of humor. We prepared a new IV for her in which we added an extra ingredient: a live gold fish. As we pretended to hook the woman up to her IV, a gold fish fluttered around in the bag. The look on the woman's face was beyond description as she saw the fish and broke out in earthshaking laughter. Someone called the local paper and our gold fish escapade made the front page of the paper the next day.

-Of caring for a beautiful child who was born without arms or legs. She was so joyful as I bathed her, splashing in the water and giggling. She also so innovatively found a way to comb her baby doll's hair by using her mouth to hold the comb and her chin and shoulder and stump of one arm to hold the doll. She found as much pleasure as any little girl would in doing those same things.

-Of being in a woman's room that had leukemia and the doctor telling her she had only a few weeks to live. She was angry and indignant saying no one could take away her hope. She changed doctors and went on to live another seven years.

-Of helping an elderly gentleman to the chair one morning who had not been strong enough to get out of bed for several days. As I bathed him with the warm soapy water, he sat in the chair too weak to help. Suddenly, he grabbed my arm and began kissing it exuberantly. "Thank you, thank you for taking care of me!" he sobbed.

- Of being present as an elderly couple renewed their wedding vows on their sixtieth wedding anniversary. They sat together holding hands on the hospital bed as platelets dripped into the bride's IV. The distinguished lady spent much of her time with us being transfused. She died a short time after.

-Of helping in the ER as a student nurse one evening and picking pieces of glass out of the forehead and cheeks of a beautiful young woman. Blood was caked in her long dark hair. She had not been wearing her seat belt and she had hit the windshield. In addition to numerous other injuries, she had lost most of her front teeth from the impact.

-Of talking to a gentleman one evening who was telling me about her new daughter-in-law and how much he loved her. The next thing he said was that his daughter-in-law was lesbian. Another family member corrected him saying "No Dad. You mean she is Lebanese."

-As a student, caring for of an elderly man who was admitted to the medical floor who had numerous maladies, severe headaches, nausea and vomiting, inability to sleep to name a few. Because I was a new student, and he was my only patient, I had the whole morning to spend with him. As we talked, I found that his wife had died three months earlier. His family in an effort to save their father further heartache, or so they thought, had taken all of their mother's belongings from the home. He said that whenever he would talk about his wife, that her children would change the subject. Consequently, the man was not given permission to grieve and also felt that a great deal of her life was invalidated. We spent time just talking. A social worker became involved to help the family realize how important it was to allow their mom to have her memories. The man was feeling much better by the end of the shift and was saved the trouble and cost of many diagnostic tests. This was my first experience in my nursing career of really feeling like I was able to make a difference and all because I had the time to listen.

-Of entering patient's room who was gazing wistfully out the window and seemed so deep in thought. When questioned she said with a straight face, "Oh I am just sitting here passing gas and contemplating the meaning of life." I guess the two could go hand in hand.

-Of seeing a fellow nurse put her hand on her back and complain that she had hurt her back. I asked how she had done it. She said that she had pulled a muscle helping the man from the funeral home transfer a body from the hospital bed to the cart to be transferred to the funeral home. I looked sympathetic and said "Boy, that'll do it. And that's dead weight!"

-Of taking care of a man who had been accidently shot in the face in a hunting accident who seemed more concerned about his partner who had shot him then about the pain and numerous reconstructive surgeries ahead.

-Of the man who told me as I placed the stethoscope on his belly to listen for bowel tones. "You know what you are hearing don't you?" he said. "No, what am I hearing?" Then he said, "UBFs." "What are UBFs?" I questioned. Then he said "Unborn Farts." I am not sure if that is a medically-approved abbreviation but it should be.

-Of a patient trying to describe her bowel habits. After about five minutes of trying to convey the frequency, consistency, color and texture, she finally said it's kind of runny and kind of not. Then she said, "I don't know what you guys call that." Impulsively I said, "Poop."

-Of a young man battling leukemia who was in intensive care. As he looked out the window, in the parking lot below was the truck of his dreams purchased by donations from family, friends and church members. Thoughts of driving that truck gave him extra incentive to fight to get better.

These are only some of the memories that have made me laugh and cry and have touched my heart.

Reverence

It is early morning and I touch my name badge to the black box and hear the familiar "beep" as the door unlatches to let me into the Cancer Center. As I walk in, the halls are empty, along with the doctor's offices, patient exam rooms and chemo suites. The only sound is a slight hum of voices from the front office staff as they are getting ready for the day.

Soon the place will come alive with people and activity everywhere. We see around 250 patients a day at our three centers. I am working in Coeur d'Alene today but have the good fortune of working at all three sites, the other two being in Post Falls and Sandpoint, Idaho.

It takes the coming together of many great people including our doctors from all corners of the world, nurse practitioners, radiation staff, certified nursing assistants, medical assistants, secretaries, chart preparation people, social workers, dieticians, pharmacists and technologists, research staff and dictation staff, information technology experts and maintenance and cleaning personnel.

Around 30 of these staff members are RNs of which I am one. I have been a nurse for 22 years now. As part of this, I have the knowledge and skills to contribute much. And for patients, I will try to be grounding a compassionate force, a resource for information, and hopefully a source of strength when they are not feeling so strong in the midst of a tumultuous cancer diagnosis.

But still the reverence for what I have the opportunity to do and observe here and at all clinics, and the outstanding coming together of each of us as we care for our patients is always with me…and I am in awe of it all!

Boots

When you are a nurse, people tell you everything and I mean everything, even things you would rather not know.

I was giving chemotherapy to a gentleman in his early 90's right before Christmas. I asked him what he wanted for Chrsitmas. He pondered a minute and then said. "Welllllll.....I need some new boots pretty bad, but you know what I really want?" "No," I said. "What do you want?" "Yoouuu knoowww!" he said with a drawl. "Oh man," I thought. "I really don't want to be going where I think this is going." Then he said, "Yeah, I told my wife what I wanted and she said, "You old fool...Go buy yourself some boots!"

Then he said, "When I was a younger lad I asked my grandfather, "When does this urge go away?" and he said, "I don't know. I'll let you know when it happens."

To laugh often and much;
To win the respect of intelligent people
and the affection of children;
To earn the appreciation of honest critics
and endure the betrayal of false friends;
To appreciate beauty, to find the best in others;
To leave the world a bit better,
whether by a healthy child, a garden patch,
or a redeemed social condition;
To know even one life has breathed easier because you have lived.
This is to have succeeded.

-Ralph Waldo Emerson-

Nellie

I met Nellie on the oncology unit about 20 years ago when I was still fairly new to nursing. The synchronistic events that lead to my discovering the rest of her story are remarkable. I have permission to write about her journey from her daughter, who is also going through treatment for cancer.

Nellie was a sweet, proud and dignified little lady who was around 78 when we first cared for her. She showed up on our unit for wound care, antibiotics, and chemotherapy. She had breast cancer. Her situation was rather unique though. Some 14 years earlier, she had noticed something beginning to grow on her breast but she kept it to herself as she did not like visiting doctors and did not want to bother anyone. I remember her telling me that her troubles were her own and she had no business bothering anyone else with them. For 14 years she hid her "trouble" as it continued to grow in size. She just kept adding padding to the other breast in an effort to disguise her tumor.

But one day while she was at a family member's home in the bathroom, the cancerous tumor burst with gangrenous foul smelling drainage running all down her front and on to the floor. That is how her secret was discovered which brought her to us.

We cleansed the wound every 8 hours. It was unlike anything I had seen in my 2 years of nursing. It was hard and lumpy and vascular with deep crevices and craters. It was very difficult to keep it clean because it kept oozing. Many times we would just let Nellie stand in the shower and have the warm water run over her breast and tumor.

This seemed to be the best way to keep up with the drainage, and it felt good to her also. Then we would pat it dry and pack the craters with a thick white cream called Silvadene that is normally used for burns. It wasn't the greatest job in the world but it was so enjoyable visiting with this sweet lady and hearing about her family. Her situation was like no other that I had ever encountered and so that made the task seem not too unpleasant.

We gave her several cycles of chemotherapy not to get rid of the cancer but to shrink it and cause it to release its grip on normal adjacent tissue, and prepare her for surgery to remove the tumor and her breast. We saw her over a period of many weeks and she was a favorite among the nurses. She eventually had her surgery and afterwards went to the surgical floor to recuperate. I lost track of sweet Nellie after that.

One day many years later, as I was giving treatment to a patient in our outpatient suite, she was telling me about her mom. I recognized the incredible story and knew immediately that it was Nellie! How remarkable to make that connection after so many years. She had had her surgery. The tumor was removed, and even after chemotherapy and attempts to shrink it, it still weighed 7 pounds.

Miraculously, the tumor was encapsulated or self-contained and had not spread anywhere else. She went on to live another 17 years and was able to be there for her grandchildren and great grandchildren living a rich and healthy life. Her daughter told me that she passed away two years earlier at age 95…

…and now I know the whole story of the proud little lady who was so determined to keep her troubles to herself.

Camaraderie II

Often when patients come to us they say things like, "Wow, I have seen this building before but I had no idea what goes on in here! It is amazing what you do and how busy you are." They comment often about how well we all seem to get along and work together. Although I have worked with so many wonderful people over the years, the team work and sense of camaraderie I feel with fellow employees here is unlike any I have ever experienced. From a practical aspect, we are all working toward one goal and that is completing all that has to be done for our patients on a daily basis, but there is much more than that.

A great deal of our success is due to the presence of our clinical supervisor of oncology services, Linda Cathey. She is the one that keeps us all united and is the glue that holds us all together. She is the greatest supervisor I have ever had. Her door is always open if there are concerns or problems. She motivates me to do my best because I feel she sees and appreciates the strengths in me and in all of us, as I see her giving her best and then some on a daily basis. She is always there with an encouraging word, a smile, and a rub of the shoulder even though many times she is under a great deal of stress herself. As our clinics grow, (there are now three) by leaps and bounds, she is right there to help. If a patient is not doing well, she is one of the first to respond. She is our liaison among physicians and all other staff. She always sticks up for us and is looking out for our best interests, and she makes us all feel like we are her favorite. She has a big job to do and she does it in a very grand way.

And as one works with other nurses so closely, there is opportunity to know how they personally would manage a situation. I see how each nurse handles the same things that I deal with daily; how they teach, how they respond to emergencies, frustrations, difficult IV starts, interacting with doctors, time management, sorrow, humor, etc. After 23 years I am still learning so much from my peers/mentors.

Many and most have gone through their own tremendous adversities; loss of loved ones, personal and family health problems, and many other tragedies. But it has only made them stronger and more compassionate. All have their own passions: faith, family, pets, fitness, education, reaching out into the community and the world, sports, hobbies, and just being passionate about living and having fun. Although all are excellent caregivers, each has their own strengths and areas in which they excel, whether it is handling emergencies, teaching, working on committees, organizing events, etc. It seems that we have all been brought together not by coincidence but by fate.

The teamwork that I experience is such an impressive coming together. Just the other day the nurses were teasing me about the black cloud that was following me all day. I had a patient that had a reaction to one of the chemo drugs and then a patient that came in with cardiac issues, two patients vomiting and numerous other things going wrong. This all could have been enough to send a nurse to the psych unit; and not as a career change.

But instead it felt much like little pieces of a puzzle all coming together to make a complete picture. During the patient's reaction, everyone showed up to help, people were recording events, getting orders from doctors, getting medications from pharmacy and administering them, nurses were doing things for my other patients, starting medications and taking chemotherapy bags down that were complete. The ill patient was stabilized as we were on to the next event.

Another gentleman came to us in distress appearing to be having cardiac issues. Everyone came on board again to help when it seemed that we had just resolved the last crisis. Labs were getting drawn and EKG's being done and meds again given and recorded. Dr's Samuels and Tezcan were there also. In the mean time, other patients were vomiting and having other problems but we were able to get everyone feeling better. By 2:00 pm I was famished and exhausted, but the second patient was stable and being transported by ambulance to our hospital.

It was a pretty intense day, but the bottom line was that it was yet another example of the incredible coming together of human spirits, each donating a part of themselves, no one trying to shine brighter than the other and, by doing that, shone brighter than any single star ever could.

Delraya and Carol RN

Chemo Queens

It's OK. You'll be fine. This happens for time to time.
You're not alone. You will see. You'll find hope with me.
It's Monday and his counts are low. Our patient's know
just where to go. Can he get his chemo? Does he need
some blood? Or just fluids this time. Anybody can be
that guy. When it happens no one knows why.
We can treat sarcoma, lymphoma or lung, and even if its breast!
So once you get your tests, come see the Chemo Queens.
We're gowned and gloved always on the scene.
Chemo Queens. Watch us work. You'll
see what we mean. Oh Yeah!
You'll be fine. He'll be fine. Reactions happen all the time.
See that nurse, make that call, quick with Demerol.
We see patients come and go. Being here is hard we know.
We care for them like family, strong through thick and thin.
So they remember when, and think of us and grin.
Because the Chemo Queens, held their
hands and renewed their dreams.
Chemo Queens, calmed their fears as
the dried their tears. Oh Yeah!
You'll be fine. He'll be fine. This happens from time to time.
See that nurse. See that guy. He is the reason why.

Words to the tune of
Dancing Queen by Abba
Written by Scherry Cripe

Scherry Cripe Certified Nurse's Assistant

To see us girls in our You Tube Video, go to
www.youtube.com and search *Chemo Queens*
Or, type in your browser
http://www.youtube.com/watch?v=p5XSViTZP8Q

The Secret

Most of us have heard of the book *The Secret*. Well, there is a well kept secret held in confidence in the medical profession. I have contemplated whether to tell it or not for quite some time, but I feel that it must be made known. It is something that most likely occurs every day across the US and around the world. And I think it is time that the public needs to know about it. It is something we all do, and I must admit that I have been known to do it at work at times myself, but I had no idea physicians did it also. The first time I saw a doctor do it, I was shocked. And I have not seen just one doctor do it, but many or most that I work with. So here it is, the great revelation that you are now being made aware of is...Doctors Google!

I knowww! It is hard to believe. I was as shocked the first time I saw it as I was the first time I saw a doctor come out of the restroom. I entered the doctor's office to ask him a question and he said, "I'm not sure" and proceeded to do a *google search* about the issue. Luckily he did not see my eyebrows raise, eyes open wide and mouth fall open because he was so into his search engine. "You mean they don't know everything!" I thought. "I could have done that!"

After I closed my mouth and composed myself, I thought about these brilliant minds I work with, and the plethora of information that must be absorbed by them that is also constantly changing. This makes it necessary to Google at times...even for them. But they know some things about googling that is very good to know. And now I am telling you.

Many times a patient will come in all fired up about something really positive or really negative that they have read on the internet or about a drug that claims to cure cancer. Web sites many times contain the opinions of the developer, and as web sites at this time have no official guidelines of evaluation, all information is not necessarily reliable. So that put the burden on the surfer to decide what is good and not so good. Here are some tips on how to evaluate credibility the medical profession knows.

1. Any site that claims that what they offer can do a number of things all the way from curing cancer to improving your sex life, to changing the oil in your vehicle is probably out to promote their own cause and fatten their own wallet more than they are interested in helping you.
2. Claims of mega doses of a product being used to cause a desired effect are probably not reputable. Usually mega doses of anything are not helpful and can even be harmful and/or toxic, and in some cases can also increase the risk of cancer development.
3. Look for correct spelling and punctuation. Errors in these categories often lend themselves to untrustworthiness.
4. What are the credentials of the author? Are their peer reviews?
5. And this is a big one! Is information presented in an objective manner offering it from a neutral unbiased point of view?
6. Look at current dates. Old, outdated information can come from dead links and be of no value.
7. How easy is the site to navigate? Are there items that require a long time to down load? Sites should be user friendly and information easy to find. (Masters, 2009)
8. Although most of us don't have access to the sites that doctors do, we can stick to well know sites such as http://www.heart.org, http://www.cancer.org/, http://www.cancer.

gov, etc. These sites are updated frequently and contain current information, facts and data.

So if you are in the exam room and your doctor is running a bit late, he may be in his office googling...or comparing your last CT scan with your current CT scan, or trying to find your lab work using three different computer systems, or waiting for a fax that contains a vital piece of information from another physician's office that is the missing link to figuring out your problem, or so many other things...Amazing creatures those doctors are, but now you know some to their secrets about successful *googling!*

Masters, K. (2009). *Role development in professional nursing practice.* Jones and Bartlett Publishers, LLC

Needie
(The Kind Voice of Bonner General Hospital)

In outpatient oncology, there is much time spent on the phone. Triaging phone calls is a very important part of what we do. We must call patients, hospitals, pharmacies, and many other facilities. Sometimes, we as nurses are on the phone 8 hours a day for several days in a row. By the last day, before you have a day off, it is a challenge. Usually by the end of the day, pharmacists and many others have snappiness in their tone, which makes the job of communicating what needs to be done that much more difficult.

But just North of Coeur d'Alene about 44 miles, in Sandpoint Idaho, there is a voice that answers with the most kindest tones and fluctuations. "Gooood Afternoon, Bonner General Hospital. How can I help you?" When you tell her what you need, you hear her say, "Certainly, one moment." I have called her number many times, at numerous times of the day, and the kindness in her voice is always there. Sometimes if someone has just beaten me up verbally in a phone call, I feel like calling the nice lady at Bonner General. I know she will always be nice to me!

A short time ago, I was working at our Sandpoint clinic, and I heard that dear voice over the intercom. I said to my coworkers, that lady is so nice. I love to talk to her. They said, "Her office is just outside that door. Do you want to meet her?" "Oh Yes!" I retorted. "I would so love that!"

We walked the short distance to where she was. There sat the same lovely lady whose voice I adored, in the flesh, taking time out of her busy day to treat me just like she always did on the phone. I told her how much her kindness meant to me. She said that she treats every interaction like it is the most important one, and that she feels so blessed having the opportunity to get to do what she loves to do each day. She feels like it is her calling, and that it is where God has put her to do His work through her.

She said that she also teaches others about her techniques and philosophies. I asked her if we could have lunch together sometime so I could learn more. We have not yet had the opportunity, but hopefully soon.

But Needie, I just want to say thank you to you for how you make me feel when I call *your* hospital. Your voice is a soothing balm on any day!

Celebrating Those That I Work With

This book is about celebrating the special moments in nursing along with who we are, and what we do.

I work with many incredible people with so many gifts, passions and talents in addition to what they do at work, and I would like to share some of these here. The following pages contain written contributions and photos from some of the marvelous people I work with.

Charlotte Mitchell Certified Nurse's Assistant at her ranch

Why I enjoy being a CNA

I started off in nursing homes night shift where after 2 weeks I told myself, "I can't do this mentally." Some patients just don't like being woke up in the middle of the night, and they let you know about it. I wouldn't like it myself.

When I started in nursing homes, I had not been around elderly much. My grandparents all passed away when I was young, so I had no idea what *they* were like, not to mention our beloved Alzheimer patients. I talked with the director and told her this and she told me to work through the weekend and I agreed to do that.

My coworkers talked to me and as the weekend was coming to an end, I had changed my mind…and that was 19 years ago; and I've never regretted that decision.

Since then, I have worked in assisted living and hospital settings and now with cancer patients, which I absolutely love. Through the years, I have seen so much. I am always asking the nurses questions. I never had a desire to be a nurse. I guess it's because I enjoy so much what I do as a CNA…and besides, all nurses love having a great assistant on the team, right?

I've always enjoyed spending time with patients, listening and helping them in whatever it is they need. I've built bonds with them. And working in an outpatient environment, I can spend more one on one time with my patients. Some of my patients are so down, and if I can put a smile on their face or even make them laugh, that is so rewarding to me. God has blessed me with a sense of humor that I can do that, even if the laugh is on me, which many times it is! You have to be able to laugh at yourself, right?

I have seen so much sadness over the years, but all the joys and rewards of my work outweigh all of that. I will continue to do what I do until I retire. I strongly feel this is where God has put me, and that must be why I enjoy what I do so much!

Charlotte Mitchell Certified Nurse's Assistant

Kim Peterson RN with husband Kelly

A God Thing

I recently took care of a patient from England. She, along with her husband had traveled to the United States to celebrate the remission of her breast cancer and also 47 years together as husband and wife. They started in San Francisco and were going to drive up to Calgary, Canada. They did all the wonderful things you do in San Francisco; Alcatraz, Fisherman's Warf, The Crookedest Street, saw the trolleys, etc. They drove up the coast through Oregon, Washington and into Idaho, where she could no longer stand the back pain that brought her into our emergency room, then to the oncology unit.

Tests showed that her cancer had not only metastasized but had spread to her bones and also her brain. She was devastated, as was her husband. Her eyes showed sorrow, but the determination of a woman who would fight it again; his eyes showed different, that of a man who knew his time with his wife was limited.

During my days off, her sons had arrived from England. By the time I returned, she had a renewed zest for life. She asked if I had seen the movie *The Bucket List*. I said that it was one of my favorite movies. She had never seen it, but her sons told her the story about how the two characters in the movie decided to make the things they wanted to do, happen in life before they died.

We talked about Jack Nicholson (who played corporate billionaire Edward Cole) and Morgan Freeman (whose role was working class mechanic Carter Chambers) became roommates at the hospital where they were getting cancer treatments. Both had poor prognoses. They decide to plug away at the things on Carter's list of things to do before he dies, and add a few more. I told her about their experience of going to Egypt to see the pyramids, and how I'd traveled to California to see the lot where they filmed that scene, and how therapeutic that movie was to me as a nurse taking care of cancer patients. My favorite scene is where Edward eats a large meal which Carter advises him against, but he thinks he knows better and does it anyway. He spends the rest of the night puking his guts out, then looks in the mirror and says, "Somewhere some lucky guy is having a heart attack."

My English friend decided she too is going to make a bucket list. Being a well to do lady, she can do many of the things she has always wanted to do, that she was always *going* to do some day, but thought she still had time. She said, "I don't know if I'll be here at Christmas, but there's a lot of things I want to do, and I'm not dead yet!" She told me of many places she wanted to go in England, Britain, and France.

But the one that made her face light up most that of going to a uniquely beautiful garden just 20 minutes from her home. She had many times planned to go there, but now was the time for her plans to become reality.

She knew she had fought this battle before, but it was going to be much harder this time. But hope gleamed in her eyes at just the thought of entering the majestic garden that she longed to witness while still her in this earthly realm. This gave her optimism about fighting her cancer one last time. She wanted to live long enough to make some memories she'd be proud of.

She talked about her kids and her grandkids and how her boys were stronger than she could have ever imagined them being; and was so proud of the fine men they'd become.

She talked of her friend that is like a sister to her, and knows her deepest secrets. One request her friend asked of her before she dies.

She wants me to take her to a restaurant in downtown England that has the most wonderful food and is simply stunning inside. This one is the best *and the most expensive* in all of England, not just anyone can afford to eat there, that's the one she wants to go to. "Can you believe that?" she chuckled. "Here I am fighting for my life, and she wants me to stay alive and take her to this bloody restaurant!" She thinks this is hilarious, and is determined to take her friend there one last time. This too gives her hope, puts a smile on her face and *lights a candle which is just beaming in her soul, radiating through her eyes.*

I have been in her room for an hour! This never happens, most nights I am lucky to get 5 or even 10 minutes to talk to a patient, if I'm lucky. As the charge nurse this night, I was assigned only 2 patients. My nurses and nursing assistants were working away; the phone didn't ring, call lights didn't go off, and no one tracked me down at this point. *This was a God thing!* He needed me to talk with this woman and help her find that hope she needed to get her home.

We talked for a half hour more when she asked jokingly, but genuinely, if I thought God would let her into heaven. "Absolutely!" I told her, "One day we would all die, but there was only two ways to die, quickly, which is swift for the person that goes, but torture for those left behind who never get to say goodbye. Or slowly, with cancer, where you can right all your wrongs, say all the things you never got to say and do the things you always wanted to do." She said, "You're right. It is like putting your life on pause from all the busy things going on that mean nothing, but tangle us up and keep us too busy to stop and see what really matters. It's like getting a second chance at life."

I encouraged her to keep a journal of the things we just talked about so that one day when she was gone, her loved ones could look back and see the hope they brought her; that just seeing the face of her kids and grandkids, and getting to hug them one more time, and lunch with her dear friend, and her sons traveling here to see her while their wives and children were at home, was giving her the strength to fight her cancer so she could get back home to England.

My nurses aid found me at this time, but I had managed to spend another half hour talking to her; an hour and a half of uninterrupted time to talk with a patient about what really mattered in life! This is virtually unheard of in nursing. I don't know if she will ever journal, or if she'll get to do all the things she wanted to do before she goes to heaven, but I know that just the thought of them gave her hope and pure joy. While all alone in a hospital room, they gave her strength to fight and embrace this one day, and face the day soon that she would have to let go.

I'll never forget this conversation with this patient. It was God intervening on both our behalf. We both needed hope that day; she to fight to see her family again and make memories that matter; and myself struggling internally with pondering changing fields in nursing. We see less and less cancer patients on our floor, as most chemo is done on an outpatient basis. My precious time with her reminded me why I became a nurse, and that God wants me to take care of His people suffering with cancer so that I may give them hope to find the things that matter to them in life. to make memories before He takes them home.

Kimberly Peterson RN

Nancy Clough RN OCN with her pack goats

Another Nurse's Story

Oncology nursing is an experience where you get to share the deepest human emotions of both fear and joy. You use some of the most exciting biotechnology available in the world, and work with the most compassionate teams ever assembled.

Oncology nursing fits my personal philosophy of doing what you can with the tools God gave you to promote a healthy life. I get to be the health promotion cheerleader and sales manager for our patients who are dealing with cancer. Our patients are dealing with the anxiety of being on a journey they did not choose, nor is the end destination known. They have an important job to do and we get to cheer them on every step they take. The rewards of this type of nursing are grand, and I would not trade them for anything.

Nancy Cough RN OCN

Wynda Dobler RN with her first grandbaby

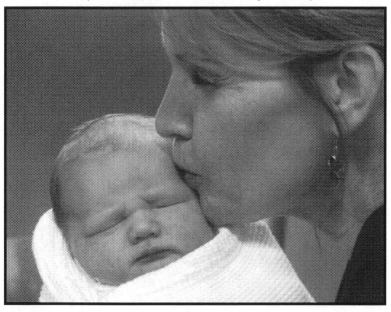

Peggy Sorenson RN OCN in costume

For the Love of Aunt Jane

Just last week, one of my patients asked me why I chose to become an oncology nurse. It wasn't the first time I've been asked that, but every time it happens it makes me stop and remind myself why I love what I do.

Back during my growing up years, I had an Aunt Jane who was diagnosed with a hereditary type of pancreatic cancer at age 27. That was in the 1960s when cancer treatment was close to barbaric and not often very effective. However, with some experimental therapies Aunt Jane did live until age 39. She managed to accomplish a lot during her short life. She was a Catholic nun, a teacher and later on left the convent and achieved a Masters degree in Library at a university not far from where she was getting her chemotherapy. She loved books and she went on to set up a library at a school nearby. Jane was a fun loving, caring, and dynamic person who lit up the room when she walked in. Her unwavering positive attitude and sense of humor made everyone she met adore her. I remember how the large Catholic Church overflowed with people the day of her funeral.

During my past 23 years as an oncology nurse, I have met a countless number of "Aunt Janes". The people I care for are an inspiration as they make the best of things while their lives are interrupted and threatened by a disease that requires them to undergo heavy duty treatments that can last for months and even years!

So, the reason I love what I do is that I can be a positive part of helping people to navigate through the long hard road that is cancer therapy. I have seen many changes in how cancer is treated since my Aunt Jane went through it. Exciting new therapies have prolonged lives and brought about cures that were unattainable 40 years ago.

As we human beings battling illness, whether it's our own or that of our loved one, I believe that there is something in life that each and every one of us needs --- *HOPE*! As I care for my patients and their families I do my best to help them keep their sense of hope alive. The most important thing I do in my work is to simply *listen*. By doing this I discover the *person* who just happens to be stuck with this disease. Everyone has a story and I learn so much from those I give treatment to. For me it is truly a blessing to be "their Nurse," and I hope that my part in their care helps to make it all a little easier.

Peggy Sorenson RN OCN

Hope

...You gotta have hope. You gotta have something.
There's always a reason to break.

Hope 'cause nothing less will save the day!

Song by Five for Fighting

Sweet Sarah

Even when she's not on duty, a nurse is still a nurse.

It was mid June 1994. My son was participating in an American Legion baseball tournament in a town in Montana. My husband and I were there as fans. We were sitting in the bleachers getting ready for the morning games to begin when some family members of one of the other young men on the team arrived. The young man's sister, Sarah, was very pregnant and appeared to be in a great deal of distress. They had arrived in Montana the day before and her labor pains had started the evening before, earlier than expected. She had spent the night at a local hospital. But even though her pains were 2 to 3 minutes apart and quite intense, they were not progressing. She was discharged from the hospital and encouraged to go to her home town hospital as soon as she could and that entailed a drive of about three and a half hours. This was her first child and although she was doing her best to try to be brave, I could tell that she was afraid.

Sarah and her mom were getting ready to head home. The plan was to meet Sarah's dad on the way at a designated location and he would take her to the hospital in a larger, more comfortable vehicle. They were leaving, but I couldn't let them go without offering to ride with them. I thought Sarah would be more comfortable with a nurse along, even though I was an oncology nurse. I could help her with some breathing techniques because she had not been able to take any birthing classes. We took off quickly and got on the freeway with Sarah's mom driving the little blue 1977 Datson pickup with bucket seats, Sarah on the console in between, her head almost hitting the roof, and myself squished against the door on the passenger side. It was a warm day so the windows were open and the road noise very loud while we whisked down the freeway at 70 miles an hour.

This was before cell phones and what did we see passing us in the opposite lane but Sarah's dad. We had missed him! We couldn't lose precious time and couldn't contact him so we just kept on. For the next three hours, and probably the longest three hours of all our lives, especially Sarah's, we persevered toward our destination.

Sarah was so brave and tried so hard to hold back the tears even though she was so uncomfortable, especially during contractions. We timed them and worked on breathing. I would rub her arm and try to massage areas of her lower back that I could reach in our cramped quarters. I tried to speak calmly when really I was thinking, "What if Sarah's water breaks? I am not an OB nurse!" The what if's were getting pretty bad as we drove on and on and the minutes ticked away and each new contraction seemed to get a little closer and a little more intense.

I was never so happy to see that blue H sign as when we pulled off the freeway that day. I breathed a tremendous sigh of relief as we headed toward the hospital. We were finally there! Sarah gave birth to Jordan Anthony just a few hours after we arrived. She was tired but did well and her new son was perfect.

A short time after, Sarah sent me a thank you card that said,

"Thank you so much for helping me through the most difficult time in my life. I consider you just as much a part of Jordan's delivery as any of the nurses. Thank you for helping bring my little angel into this world!"

I ran into Sarah and her mom a short time ago. With them was a tall young man just as handsome as Sarah is beautiful. It was Jordan!

He is now 13 and loves baseball too. His grandmother relayed the story of my small part in helping with his arrival. As he greeted me with a warm smile and extended his hand to shake mine, I thought to myself...

"Even when she's not on duty...it's great to be a nurse!"

Hit the Road Jack

"Be it declared to all present that *Joe Miller* having completed the prescribed course of Chemotherapy with a high order of proficiency in the Science and Art of being cheerful, outstanding in high courage, tolerant and determined in all order given, is therefore now entitled to receive certification as an active member in our 'FAVORITE PATIENT CLUB' subject to all rights, honors and privileges."

That is what it says on the certificate signed by all the nurses, certified nursing assistants and whomever is around on that particular day. We present this to the patient along with a booklet entitled *"Life After Cancer Treatment."* Although it is a desired outcome to get to the end of their treatment, chemotherapy has been their lifeline, or more appropriately their bungee cord. There are so many ups and downs, and I would imagine that one has the feeling that their head will smash into the ground.

Also, they are ending their relationships with all of us who have been there to give them not only their treatment but support and most importantly, friendship. They wonder, "Will I be ok? What do I do now? How should I expect to feel?" The booklet helps address some of these issues. We also present them with a small decorated cake as we say farewell.

Afterwards, we all sing, "Hit the Road Jack and don't cha come back no more, no more, no more, no more……" followed by hugs from all.

I have been met with many reactions to the above scenario. Sometimes the individual on the receiving end looks surprised, begins dabbing their eyes, sobs, laughs, or looks to be full of pure joy at having completed this with all the courage, anger, hope, and ambivalence that it has taken.

My last experience was with a ruggedly tough older gentleman who was very fidgety as I read the words on the certificate. I thought that he was just anxious to be done and just wanted out. He then said, "I don't know what to do. I'm not used to this attention." I said, "This is your time. Just enjoy the moment. You have earned it." He stood up and we all hugged and congratulated him. As he reached into his back pocket to pull out a wadded handkerchief, a fat tear escaped from its tear duct and gently rolled down his cheek when he caught it midway with the wrinkled cloth. He was unable to say anything else, but no other words were needed as the man left the clinic.

We dabbed our own eyes, and were grateful for making the effort to come together that meant so much to this man. I heard a patient say the other day, "I can't wait till they sing 'Hit the Road Jack' to me."

So, as I come closer to completion of this writing, I pray that each of you that have taken the time to read this, find the strength to move forward through the difficulties of life, the courage to take the steps through the door that lead to the unknown, and discover the joy that awaits you as you move ahead.

Conclusion

May I always be mindful of the pride that I feel being in this profession and never take this gift for granted or the responsibility lightly. May I never lump people together according to their diagnosis or malady. May I see them as individuals with hopes and lives and dreams and loved ones as important as I feel mine are. May I speak of them when they can't hear my words just as if we were talking face-to-face. May my tone of voice and mannerisms, as well as the words I speak portray acceptance, support and confidence. May my knowledge base be solid and ongoing, my assessments be accurate and my teaching be useful and well received. May my touch be gentle and my hand be steady. May I treat each person whose care I am entrusted with as I would my own loved one. May I see divinity in each life I care for. These are the goals for which I continue to strive.

And that is my story!

(Top row) Teena, Chris, Charlotte
(Bottom row) Cynthia, Pam, Lisa, Peggy, Delraya
Surprise birthday party at work for Peggy's 60th.